SLAYING CONFLICT HEALING SOULS

Are We There Yet?

Five Steps to Real Peace Now

Eric Lo

Exulon
ELITE

Praise for *Slaying Conflict, Healing Souls. Are We There Yet?*

"Conflict is inevitable" says this book. As a physician, I know how true this statement is and how unresolved personal conflict can adversely affect one's mental, physical, and spiritual health.

"Are we there yet?" makes Biblical based conflict resolution easy to understand by using the allegory of a car trip with fictional animal characters who have personal problems to face. While they are traveling from Securatown to Everland, the reader finds out how these characters discover the nature of their conflicts and learn from Wise-owl a practical "toolbox" of ideas on how to address them.

Whether you are a pastor, layman, or healthcare professional you will very much enjoy this book and discover many simple ways to understand what is under laying the cause of conflict, techniques on addresses them, and what outcomes to expect from your efforts. This is a book that those who deal with unresolved conflict would greatly benefit from and I plan to make it available to the patients in my medical practice.

Harry Drummond, MD Chairman,
Department of Family Medicine
Simi Valley Hospital, California

Eric Lo's new book, *Are We There Yet?* projects itself like a fast-paced animation film on the screen of our imagination, while playing its script as a subconscious soundtrack to our intelligence. What happens in our minds and hearts is the real story of this book. We come to realize that the characters are such close reflections of our own minds and personalities that we want to become better characters.

By the time the book reaches the end of the journey, we realize that the inner child riding in the back seat of our mind really enjoyed the trip!

Major C. Patrick Granat
Regional Commander for
The Salvation Army in Poland

Over the past week, I've read your book twice. It's wonderful. I found it to be engaging, instructive, practical, touching, inspiring… and more. I congratulate you sincerely on what I am convinced will be an enormously helpful resource for anyone who has ever experienced conflict – in short, everyone!

I think that the sentence which made the greatest impact on me was this: "In conflict, you stand toe to toe with who you are, who you are not, and who you want to be." To my mind, that's not only an accurate understanding of conflict, but it's also one of the best reasons for placing your faith in Christ. After all, once you understand who you truly are, you're immediately aware of how much you need Him!

Commissioner Kenneth G. Hodder
INTERNATIONAL SECRETARY
FOR PERSONNEL (LONDON, ENGLAND)

I thoroughly enjoyed the opportunity to read and review the book "Slaying Conflict Healing Souls, Are We There Yet?" This is an exceptional read with beautiful ideas on how one can manage through conflict in a Christ-like manner. Major Lo has done this in a creative but practical manner. The reader will value the author's insights and when applied, the steps to real peace will absolutely support the cause of the seeker.

This book and its contents have my heartfelt endorsement. I recommend it for the individual who is facing conflict and for the support person who is helping someone to move through it.

May God bless you as you allow the Holy Spirit to speak to you through these pages.

James M. Knaggs, Commissioner
TERRITORIAL COMMANDER

This book is a masterpiece with original and inspired idea. It is a compulsory read to all irrespective of our current position in the journey of life. I wish Eric the greatest success in his life and many more books to come.

Gary Law Major,
Commanding Officer 2381 BCR (Irish Fusiliers)
RCACC Corporal, Pro-Active Recruiting NCO.
Royal Canadian Mounted Police

Conflict transformation requires an honest look at reality as it is not as we imagine or like it to be. *Are we there yet?* Captures key concepts in working with conflicts with down to earth real life examples and easy to remember steps for application. It also reflects the author's honest and deep interior journey of self-transformation. It can make you laugh, smile, sob, or sigh. Not only it is good food for the soul, it is an easy read and a must read for pastors and mediators.

Rev. Dr. James K. Law,
certified mediator and senior pastor
of Chinese United Methodist Church, New York.

As an author, I like to say "every good book is a love story." If a person loves flowers, that person might write a book about flowers. If a person loves golf, he may write a book about how to develop the perfect swing.

My book, "Breakfast At Sally's," is a love story about life. I wanted to end my life because I was homeless. Now I want to live forever because people find my book inspiring and life-changing.

Eric Lo's book "Are We There Yet?" is a love story, too. He uses his sense of humor and creativity as he gives us five steps to slay conflict and heal our souls. Like any good book Eric's work takes the reader to places where the reader begins to apply his words to their life.

That includes me. I found myself seeking ways to face and heal the conflicts in my own life. That is a tribute to Eric's words.

Eric's book can change lives. I recommend that everyone read his book. I give it five stars!

Richard LeMeux, author "Breakfast At Sally's,
One Homeless Man's Inspirational Journey"

Eric's material is both "profound and simple". He has presented profound conflict resolution techniques utilizing a simple story format which helps the reader to immediately apply the presented strategies. This short book is a practical guide to dealing with conflict in a healthy and God-honoring way. An added bonus are the "Let's Huddle" group discussion questions at the end of the book that correspond with each chapter. An encouraging and enlightening read for pastors, leaders, and well,–just people. Because, let's face it… We all, at times, face conflict.

Linda E. Manhardt, Major Training Principal
The Salvation Army Officer Training
College Philippines MA (marriage,
family and child counseling)

Out of his decades of immersion in the daily demands of ground-level, gut-level encounter with the humanness and sometimes, 'cussedness' of our interactions, even within the fellowships of God's people, Major Eric Lo has distilled an invaluable treasury of workable insights for dealing with conflict and moving toward reconciliation. Nothing brings greater pain to the heart of God than our inability to love our way through our hurts and disagreements. The stakes are high for the credibility of our witness as the reconciled and redeemed people of God in the brokenness of our world. *Slaying Conflict, Healing Souls, Are We There Yet?* is a clever and colorful presentation of practical steps toward understanding and action. It is an excellent resource for study and discussion in our Corps and churches.

Paul A. Rader General (Ret.)
The Salvation Army

"Are We There Yet?" is an intriguing work. It is written in a uniquely simply yet sophisticated, edgy but enjoyable style. Far from "preaching" at the reader, this book draws us in, excites our thinking processes and encourages each of us to reach and appreciate our own conclusions. Just as silence sometimes speaks the loudest and teaches the most, the gaps that are unwritten in this book enticed me to make important observations on life and discoveries about my own character. The uncomplicated, beguiling language contains great wisdom; it draws out the explorer and adventurer in each of us. "Are We There Yet?" is a fun, profound and meaningful read!

Chief Kathleen Sheehan
Port Hueneme Police Department California

This book has a down to earth, authentic and practical approach in dealing with conflict in daily life. I would particularly recommend that it be available in college libraries.

Cecilia Tobin, retired teacher
New Zealand

I have a wonderful time reading *Are We There Yet?* It was as if listening to classical music by the Masters.

I love the fable style he chose to write this hard subject of "conflict management'; a tough art to master, let alone read about it. For me, the secret of enjoyment of reading is "a meeting of two minds"; the reader's and the writer's. The best condition to read is when the writer is having a heart to heart conversation with the reader. Much like being courted in a romance. Then the reader will comprehend what's been written, and will internalize the messages. This will lead to transformation of the mind. The writer's intention is achieved through this manner of sharing his passion and experience. My soul is healed. Glory be to God."

Betty Lee Lo, Managing Director, Citibank
Private Bank,
Asia Pacific, Singapore

Happy customers and contented employees are the goal of every business. Managing conflict is a key part of the equation. This book has given me a goldmine of conflict resolution skills through relevant situational examples and solutions. I found it easy to read and understand, entertaining and effective.

Monica Rogers, Full of Peppers LLC

In the journey of life and ministry, we travel with others. This reality brings moments of deep joy and inevitable moments of painful conflict. This book captures that reality in a fable approach to the story, with lessons that can easily be applied to life's journey. I am pleased to endorse this book as a tool to understand conflict, ourselves and a healthy and biblically-sound response.

This is a book that can be read and used individually and also as a resource for any leadership team to share.

The content is enriched with exercises for reflection and group learning.

Commissioner Floyd J Tidd, The Salvation Army
Australia Southern Territory

Eric Lo's clever use of allegory helps get past the defenses we put up when discussing the difficult subject of conflict. You will recognize in the characters, people you know, and have encountered in ministry. The "names have been changed to protect the innocent" (and some who are not too innocent)! A helpful new take on a timeless topic.

Colonel Mark Tillsley, Ph.D Chief Secretary
The Salvation Army Canada and Bermuda Territory

This practical and insightful resource will be useful for everyone. It is simple and easy, not only to understand, but apply in any kind of relationship. This book does not over-whelm you, but leaves you with the feeling, 'This material makes sense and I can do this!'"

Dr. H. Norman Wright Marriage, Family & Child
Therapist. Author of over seventy books.

Dedicated to

All of us who have been touched by conflict,
And to those who help me transform it;
My Lord Jesus,
My wife Cheryl, our children, Ethan and Bethany,
And our grand-daughter, Kalia Gallagher

In a land not far away
Where dogs are racist
And cats aren't welcome to stay
John goes on a journey
And Wise-owl guides his way

It's the worst of times
When hate reaches 9/11
It's the best of times
When love triumphs over getting even

So take the journey of conflict, hope, and dread
It's a journey long neglected
And we often ask, "Are we there yet?"

Table of Contents

Tools you can use

Foreword

Reading through the manuscript of *Slaying Conflict, Healing Souls, Are We There Yet?* I found myself pleasantly surprised. Frankly, I was suspecting another heady, boring but necessary textbook type treatise on conflict management. It was quite the opposite, thankfully.

Creatively written, it reads like a feature film, acts, scenes, plot points and all, and written in intriguing allegory form. The author notes that this book was "written in a foxhole," and boy, as a Salvation Army pastor, leader, husband, father and all around human being, could I resonate with those foxhole experiences. Now retired, where was this book when I needed it?

I was amazed at how much wisdom and life experience could be captured in such easy, fast-paced read. It was fun too. For example, one stop on "Are We There Yet" journey is Cowpalace, home of Mad Cow, Sacred Cow, Beefy Cow, Milky Cow and Holy Cow. Now if this doesn't conjure up images of conflict, nothing will. The "fun" part is in discovering how it all gets resolved.

What also makes this book unique is the "Road Signs" along the way giving guidance, direction and clarity. Are you there yet? No, but the signs in this book, if followed, will help get you there. A must read for anyone who has ever or who will ever experience conflict. That's everyone!

Joe Noland Commissioner
The Salvation Army

Author's note

Conflict. We all have someone or know someone who has been wounded by it. Perhaps you are the one hurting. Silence is not golden when we are in pain.

I would not have written a book on *conflict* in a million years, but some nice, religious, and spiritual churchgoers ambushed me, my wife, and our small children. In our own church. Our own people.

We had to put a shatter-proof glass window on our free clinic after our nurses received threats of violence.

The police picked up a teenager from our church cutting his wrist because of bullying at school.

A bitter divorce had torn apart one of our best workers, a true professional.

The dreams and ambitions of our children clashed with our ideas, ending in explosive words, sleepless nights, and grey hairs.

In seeking counsel, I was surprised to learn how many have similar problems, or worse. The young, the old, the rich, the poor, the friend, the boss, the employee. More people are hurting than you know.

After thirty years as pastor, administrator, and peacemaker, my pursuit to understand conflict has become a second burning bush experience. I am compelled by a mission.

I have read over a hundred books dealing with conflict, attended seminars, and became certified as a mediator.

In some way, writing this book has forced me to confront my own nagging internal conflict also: "You want to do what? A foreigner who has flunked English as a second language? A skinny boy who wants to beat a Sumo wrestler?"

The battle scars and the *Aha* moments have served me well. They have enabled me to merge a national organization's local chapter with The Salvation Army local chapter, resurrect a church under legal fire, and reclaim peace for many wounded souls through my Agapeace peacemaking ministry.

The stories I hear from common and not-so-common people are incredible.

With collective tears and hope as my ink, I have written this in the foxhole, the confusing place where we hope there is a guide to find a way out, and somebody to grab us by the hand and say "Can I help? I will listen with respect, without judgment, and keep it confidential."

Inside conflict is an unfolding story, so I have used a fable with six Acts to tell it. Each Act in this drama addresses one aspect of conflict resolution-defining, responding, triaging, decoding, managing, and transforming conflict.

In this brief and easy read, you will find tools you can use, hope you can hang on to, and an encouraging pat on the shoulder you can pass along.

May your load and theirs be lightened as you journey in the land of "Are we there yet?"

Road Sign

"In the end, we will remember not the words of our enemies, but the silence of our friends." Martin Luther King Jr.

Act 1:

The Journey Begins—Defining Conflict.

Act 1: Scene 1: Life Is Good Until . . .

John is so nice that, wherever he is, he becomes a fire-hydrant in Dog City.

At the moment, another blustery day will soon say good-bye to Securatown. In a few hours, the setting sun will be ready to tuck its people into bed. All is peaceful, secure, predictable.

John stretches out on his favorite leather recliner, turning up a bit the volume of Neil Diamond's "Longfellow Serenade," and slurping a cup of steaming hot Jasmine tea, with lemon. What a great Sunday afternoon!

Nancy and Sarah are attending the women's conference fifteen- hundred miles away, having a much needed mother-daughter time away from the skirmishes over a messy room and lousy friends.

His dog Buddy cuddles around his feet, Wise-owl, his trusted pet and teacher dozes off while clinging onto the swing hanging from the ceiling. Except for Fluffy the cat, who is nowhere to be found, everyone is in the living room, in their usual places, eyes closed, smiling.

Better that way. Separating the dog and the cat from constant fighting is more than a chore. Particularly lately.

Then the phone rings.

"No. Not the church people again, please."

These last three months since John arrived as new pastor to the First Securatownian Church, tension has smelled like rotten fish in a new refrigerator. There have been church fights over who uses the coffee pot, who spills the beans, and who lets the dogs out.

The parishioners grill him and his family over religious fire in unofficial church picnics. The menu includes his sermons, songs, Levi jeans, and not taking the ladies out to lunch on Mother's Day.

A few have written anonymous letter to his bishop demanding his head on a platter. They lust for his blood. But why?

Even if there is a crime at all, does it deserve such punishment? Where do all these come from? And where do they all belong?

He has just left a church that loved them dearly. The special farewell poems, the cards, and the gifts still make him smile, sadly.

Being a nice guy who always wants to get along with people, he wishes things will go away. But things don't go away. They're getting worse. And worse.

Ring, ring, ring. He picks up the phone.

Act 1: Scene 2: Conflict is Inevitable.

"Oh no... I'll be there"

"What's wrong, John?" Wise-owl asks.

"My dad's in a coma. Few days to live," he mumbles to himself while rubbing his forehead, "God, if only I had told him. . ."

To say anything meaningful across twelve hundred miles is hard. The childhood nightmare seems to have faded in these twenty-five years since leaving Everland. But if he can't tell dad his secret, his dad will never have another chance. He needs to resolve this.

And the problem is not the childhood nightmare.

"Wise-owl, I need to take off right away. Can you go with me? I wonder if Nancy and Sarah should. . . Well, no. I shouldn't cut short their conference. Nancy is one of the speakers and can meet me at the hospital. I need to do some thinking, anyway. You can go with me, right?"

"Of course!

"What about Buddy and Fluffy? They fight like dogs and cats. It's a two days' trip."

"It'll be worse if they stay here by themselves. To find a kennel open Sunday night is impossible. Besides, you have taken them for long trips before." Wise-owl says.

"I worry my aunt and uncle will show up. Between me and Uncle Robert, there is still some scar tissue."

"Even if John wears a royal gown, he wouldn't look like a prince." After thirty-five years that remark from Robert, turning up his nose at his mom, still stings.

Was that because he was not someone born bright, sharp and confident? Or was it because his dad couldn't put food on the table, trapped by compulsive gambling?

These are questions long forgotten.

"But, John, conflict is part of life. You'll be *okay*. I will bring some tools along to help."

Act 1: Scene 3: The Way We Were.

John takes ten minutes to pack a small suitcase, but way past midnight he is still unpacking and re-packing the pain, doubts, and memories of yesterday—memories of living in a ghetto, his absentee father, and his snobby aunt and uncle.

Was that why he left Everland and went across the country to find fortune and peace?

What if he had confronted his dad when he mistreated his mom, and had dealt with Robert when he treated his family with contempt?

What if he had not been so timid, but more assertive?

Being always considerate of other's feelings, he wouldn't do anything that would make people uncomfortable, but why wouldn't others consider his feelings for a change?

John has no answers, only questions and regrets. But he knows he is likely to run into his extended family in a few days. How can someone shy and non-confrontational handle this? He hates being a push-over.

The clock is ticking, ready or not.

Act 1: Scene 4: Into the Heart of Conflict.

T he sun has risen finally after a long sleepless night. The ride has just begun, but it already seems an eternity, overloaded with heavy cargo. The scenic drive along Highway 56 is beautiful and relaxing, but John's internal journey is anything but relaxing.

As usual, he worries and analyzes too much.

Wise-owl reads his mind. "John, let's start by accepting conflict as unavoidable and as natural as fish swimming in the water, and let's understand what conflict is."

"What is conflict?"

"Conflict is the creature that finds its way into an unresolved anxiety when the container is smaller than the stuff being contained. When the space is smaller than the occupant. When more than one stands in the space just big enough for one."

"What do you mean by container and stuff, space and occupant? You've lost me."

"Let me show you," Wise-owl answers. With a few flaps of his wings, he squeezes himself between Buddy and Fluffy in the back seat.

"You are crowding me." Buddy and Fluffy exclaim in unison, the only time they have seemed united on this trip.

"See this seat? That's the container, and the stuff is Buddy, Fluffy, and me. Like sardines, we are squeezed and packed in the container. Now we have a conflict. Right?"

Wise-owl jumps back to John, smoothing out his wings a bit and straightening his oversized glasses.

"Remember, stuff or occupants are not necessarily just things. Stuff can be a need, a position, value, thought, expectation, idea, assumption...etc.

The container or space is not only a thing either. It can be something physical, mental, or emotional. A mind-set is a typical mental container."

"Wise-owl, this is helpful. Can you explain more?"

"Sure. Most conflict is not about right or wrong, but about the intolerance of differences, or the lack of appreciation and respect. I like blue and she likes purple. What's the right color?

In other words, something, someone, or some idea is not fitting into our physical, emotional, or mental space."

"I never thought about conflict this way before."

"No problem. Just simply that, putting a rigid container and an oversize occupant together will spark anxiety. If anxiety is not resolved, the spark can turn into a fire."

"But sometimes it will go away. Will it?" John asks. He has convinced himself many times with this hope and kicked himself many times afterward.

"I agree. Conflict can dissipate by itself sometimes, either because the situation has changed, or the key players have changed. Conflict may become less important due to new goals, priorities, or different moods of the main parties.

This latent conflict is what I call *cold conflict*. Yes, you can choose not to deal with it. In fact, there are times when it is best not to deal with it."

John looks puzzled, but Wise-owl continues. *"Man wants to tell, woman likes to be heard." Must be true with owls too*, John figures.

"Remember, also, conflict doesn't always have to be something between you and others. It can be an internal battle you rage against yourself, feeling torn between two ideas, at odds with your needs and wants, or not being able to reconcile your past belief with the present reality. You believed you can fly, but now you can only swim."

"It's a bit abstract. Hard to put a handle on it," John says.

"Don't worry. I'll give you some examples later. Perhaps you can come up with some yourself.

By the way, if conflict means an occupant bigger than the container, then the solution is?" Wise-owl pauses, and then answers his own question. "Increase or reshape the space, shrink or remove the occupants. Something you should think about."

Hmmmmm. Shrink Uncle Robert, like the movie *Honey, I Shrunk The Kids* ©. Though his church people still dominates John's thoughts, they begin to fade as he prepares to visit his dad, his uncle, and his past. He is exploring new ways to increase space and shrink occupants, lost in the fantasy land.

Isn't it why people look at their rivals and imagine them wearing Mickey Mouse underwear? Or what they would look like at age eight or eighty? Isn't it why negotiators study their opponents before they negotiate? Isn't this a way of shrinking to level the playing field? A light bulb has just turned on.

On the other hand, if he can expand his tolerance and accept his daughter's youth culture, they may get along better. He remembers Mary Engelbreit's saying, "If you don't like something, change it. If you can't change it, change the way you think about it."

"Have I failed my daughter?"

Seems just like yesterday when Sarah was a toddler. He must have read *Good Night Moon* © twenty times to her while holding up a flashlight in their tent castle. Then he rushed to burn midnight oil to finish the budget after she slept.

He handled anything remotely dirty with gloves on, but without a murmur or being asked, he changed her diapers or caught her worms wiggling in the backyard. He danced with his Cinderella while his body was aching for rest.

He liked being the dad he was becoming. . . .until she spilled her milk, until she insisted on having ice-cream. Until one day.

Crash! The glass castle went tumbling down.

He has warned Nancy and Sarah not to play too roughly while they tickled each other and giggled near the glass cabinet full of collector bells. They were too busy having fun.

Sarah ran for her life and hid in mommy's arms. His screaming, yelling lecture was too much.

"Are these more important than our daughter?" his wife asked. They both wept.

The whole concept of stuff and container opens up new way to see and respond to conflict. From now on, he can look at the world in terms of boxes and occupants.

"Now, how should I go about seeing my family?" he asked. "What about the church? I want to get along. You say you are going to give me some examples?"

Wise-owl welcomes John back to earth. "Most of what we are talking about can equally apply to situations at home, at work, or at church. A wheel is a wheel whether it is a wheel for a bike, or a truck, or the wheel of fortune.

"I know you have gone through a lot these few months in Securatownian. So let's use the church as example."

"That's great." John says. "This church causes me so much grief. First time I've faced so serious an onslaught in twenty years of being a pastor." John shakes his head, tightening his lips, shuddering at his own admission.

"When you started using contemporary songs in this traditional congregation, you started a conflict. They have a mental space for the traditional, but not for the contemporary. They began to grumble, right?"

"Yes, but they didn't tell me that. They just talked about me in the parking lot, or at someone's house after church."

"That's normal with people who can't handle anxiety in a healthy manner. It's called *triangulation*. We'll talk more about that later."

"Promise?" *What on earth is triangulation,* he wonders.

"Promise." Wise-owl says, "Another common church fight issue is leadership style. You want to lead, but they like being managed. Do you see a conflict here?" Wise-owl pauses.

John answers, "Yes. The stuff can't fit in the space."

"Exactly."

"I really hate conflict and try to be nice to everyone, but I wish I could speak my mind about the way I see things. Why can't I do that in the church?"

"Because of misunderstood beliefs like 'judge not' and 'blessed are the peacemakers,' and 'let whoever is without sin cast the first stone.' Then they remind everybody you are the pastor. Right?

"There is a big difference between appeasements, "Please, please, with sugar on top," and peacemaking, "if I divide the pie, you can choose which piece you like.

"Without a good sense of what the difference is, it's easier to avoid, ignore, deny, or suppress conflict than to deal with it."

"But shouldn't I turn the other cheek?" John asks.

"Not exactly. This is oversimplifying scriptural belief. It often gives the bystanders an excuse to look the other way." Wise-owl sounds a bit abrupt.

"Don't confuse loving with excusing, forgiving with denying. Most do so in the name of being spiritual. They let the most vocal criticizers and power brokers continue to roam at will, manipulating the players, while good people are seething inside. They are losing their weaker brothers and sisters to those who dare to be self-absorbed.

"Often the bystanders are unaware or want to be unaware that below the niceness hides great anxiety. The elephant in the room. They play the harmonious dishonesty game, a power play in disguise.

"Remember the movie Bambi©?"

"Yes. What about it?" John asks.

"Thumper's mom says 'if you can't find anything nice to say, don't say anything at all'. Sometimes that's poor advice. Love your people? Yes, but you must also speak the truth in love."

"I wonder, is conflict is a good thing?" John says.

"It depends. It's just inevitable. Without conflict, there will be no stories, no inventions, and no civilization. No nightly news."

John watches nothing but the news: voices of yesterday tell him he should make people like him, not rock the boat, and maintain harmony at all costs, seem but people can get along and be happily dead.

Wise-owl says, "Conflict puts you in the crossroad between destruction and creation. On the upside, it can spark social change, stop injustice, redress the wrong, and rebalance the power that has lost its restraint. It can bring about redemption, justice, kindness, forgiveness, creativity, and compassion, like Rosa Park.

"On the personal side, conflict tests and tempers our soul. If we really listen to the pain of all sides, including ours, it will tell us what we don't want to hear but need to know.

"In conflict you stand toe to toe with who you are, who you are not, and who you want to be. Conflict comes from our refusal to see or accept the things as they are."

John looks past Wise-owl, letting go a deep breath.

"Conflict ebbs and floods in a relationship, in an organization, and even within our own mental and emotional fortresses. If we see no conflict in a relationship, in an organization, or within our own thoughts, we need to suspect that we are dying or already dead."

We've never argued in our fifty years of marriage. Hmmm.

Wise-owl says, "Remember the beautiful beaches, canyons, and mountains. Where do they come from? Conflict, of course. Nature uses it to create these beautiful landmarks."

Wise-owl is right. John thinks. Geography lessons have taught him how the physical stress in the course of changing times and unfolding space has given birth to some awesome scenery. The rugged Grand Canyon, the peaceful Crater Lake, and Niagara Falls, are just gorgeous.

John says, "But I hate to stir up the pot, or fight my way out."

"You don't have to. Remember that." With a pause, Wise-owl takes out a big piece of paper and writes:

Conflict is inevitable,
Combat is optional,
Collaboration is optimal,
And . . .

"Thanks. I will remember that." John says, with a smile. Noticing the dots, he asks "what's after and . . . ?"

"I'll let you know later. Better yet, you can find out yourself."

Road sign

In conflict, you see who you are, who you are not, and who you want to be.

Check Compass

We all have conflict. What's my biggest regret?
Am I ready to take the journey of conflict transformation?

Act 2:

Dogsville—Responding to Conflict.

Act 2: Scene 1: The Not So Great Escape.

"**A**re we there yet?" Fluffy asks, making a loud-speaker with her paws.

"Of course not, you stupid cat!" Buddy answers. "Why don't you stop meowing, for a change?"

Eight hours into the ride with empty stomachs and full bladders.

"I don't want to get stuck in a car." Fluffy says. "You are pathetic. All you know is hang around John like a leash. Can't you think or do anything on your own? Anything?"

John can hear the hissing teeth and swinging claws of these two intimate enemies.

"You two stop fighting, or I'll chain you up." John says, steering his mini-van along the picturesque but bumpy highway. "Two more hours, and we'll be in Dogsville to get something to eat."

"Oh no," Fluffy says. "I've heard they don't like cats. They say we are inferior. They brag about dozens of ways to skin a cat. Let's take another route, please."

"No. It will take us three extra hours to go around Dogsville. Besides, that's racism. It's wrong."

John aches at his own comment, reliving the painful visit with a church member two months ago. The shock and hurt he felt when David told him, "Mark is a redneck. He doesn't want you to be pastor of this church."

John had felt pain before, but that was the worst. For God's sake, this happens at a church. His own church.

"John, Fluffy is right. Let's take another route," Wise-owl says.

"You see, there are five ways you can respond to conflict. Right now, the best way is to avoid it. Let me pull out a chart to show what I mean by that."

Wise-owl jumps into the back of the van, opens his old beat-up brief case, and comes back with the chart.

Needs determine fit

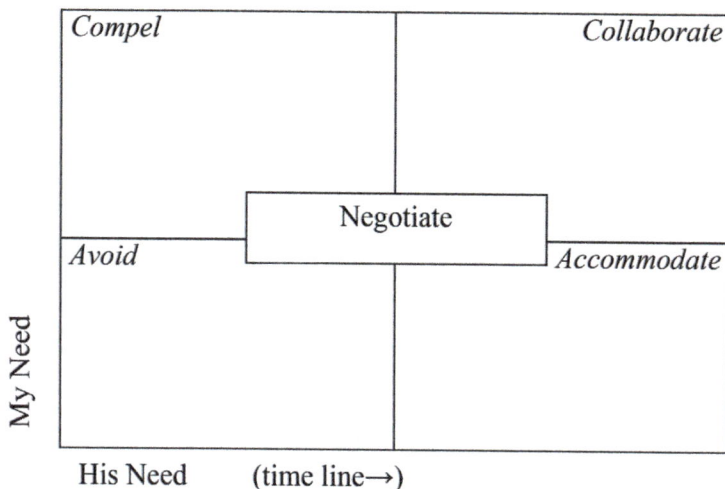

Compel		Collaborate
	Negotiate	
Avoid		Accommodate

My Need

His Need   (time line→)

"You see, responding to conflict boils down to balancing what you want with what they want. To a lesser degree, how much time you have to deal with it matters."

Under the chart, Wise-owl pencils these words:

Needs determine fit

"Seems a lot to digest." John replies. His favorite pastime is chewing up information.

"Not really, once you understand the chart. You can see the response in your head." Wise-owl says.

"Let's say you really don't care about the other guy's need. If you have the ability, you can **compel** or force him to do what you want. Your response will be in the top left corner—*compel*. The time needed will be short. You just tried to compel Buddy and Fluffy to behave, didn't you?

Wise-owl points to the left lower corner. "But if both meeting your need and their need is low, the response is in the lower left corner; *Avoid.*"

"So," John says, narrowing his eyes, "we should avoid Dogsville because going through Dogsville and dealing with racism is not that important for now, and the time to deal with it is short?"

"Yes. Let's see how it works in a different *avoid* or *compel* situation. Let's say that in the middle of the night, someone breaks into your house. How do you respond?"

John says, "I know he and I don't have a personal relationship, or need one. Time to resolve the problem is short, my need of safety is high, and I don't care about his need. Now, if I have a gun, I have the upper hand, and I can compel him to leave. But if he has the upper hand, I need to avoid him."

"Yes. And how do you avoid him?"

"I guess hide behind the closet, under the bed, or lock myself in the basement or—"

"You are right. But remember, avoidance is only one of the five responses, and it shouldn't become a way of life. We can't always walk away from conflict or sweep things under the rug."

Wise-owl takes a long pause. "You know, after twenty-five years, you still dodge your aunt and uncle, and to some degree avoid your father as well."

John nods, holding his breath.

"Conflict doesn't just evaporate. It submerges, but comes up at the worst time. Ever try pushing a Ping-Pong ball under water? Once you remove your hand, it will pop up again, right?"

"I'll remember that. What about the other responses on the chart?" John skims over this one fast.

"You mean *negotiate, accommodate,* and *collaborate*?"

"Yes."

"Since we are talking about racism in Dogsville, let's continue with this example, only this time you are living in Dogsville, not passing through."

"Does it mean the time to deal with it is longer?"

"You got it. Besides, it is your city. You live there and build relationships there. Now, what are your needs and their needs?"

"My need is to see that racism goes out the window, because cats should have equal rights. I guess the dogs' need is to get rid of the cats because they hate cats.

"Maybe the dogs hate the cats because they see something they don't like about themselves in the cats?"

Wise-owl grins. "*Hmmm* . . . good thoughts."

"Another thing, John. Racism is the sad thing mushrooming out of the shadowy pit of fear of the unknown, laziness of the mind, and timidity of the heart. We had better enlighten those minds and hearts before they turn totally dark and callous.

"The sad thing is that most people don't want to deal with racism because it pokes at our fear and ignorance. It requires hard honest work to overcome. So they miss out on genuine relationships and many good things in life that are theirs for the taking."

"Wise-owl, it strikes me that in many ways, racists are lazy. They don't want to think. For them, it's much easier and faster to lump every individual into a group. It resembles indexing, labeling, and packaging in the supermarket. Managers profile the needs of the customers, and manufacturers mass-produce the goods for the shelves, to make a profit.

"But human beings are not goods, nor logic machines. How can we think like that?" John is talking to himself.

"John, we all do it at times for convenience when we are in a hurry or in a stressful situation. Sometimes it's just easier to put people in a box we know than in a box we don't. We don't care enough, or we are too afraid to invest time to know others.

"You have heard that dogs are loyal, cats are carefree, and pigs are lazy. Are they really? Or those just our callous thoughts?

"Now that you live in Dogsville, you can invest time to deal with racism. You can move towards negotiate, accommodate, or collaborate." Wise-owl straightens out the chart again.

"Think about this. Remember the thief at night in your room? What if it turns into a hostage situation? Police will barricade the building; buy more time, and make one of the five responses. Guess what that is?"

John has the answer on the tip of his tongue.

Wise-owl looks out the window, and gives John a chance to think. He turns back, and points to the chart, and says,

"When the need to meet both your need and their need is high, you **collaborate.** When meeting your need is low priority and their need is high priority, you **accommodate.** Right in the middle, you **Negotiate.**"

Wise-owl pauses, remembering some bad experiences.

"Negotiation is often used in hostage situations."

"Why is that?" John asks.

"In negotiation, you both try to balance gains and losses, keep things settled for the time being, and move on. You hope to resolve the situation quickly, but both collaboration and accommodation are evolving processes, and you are there for the long haul.

As long as you are in a relationship, at home, at work, or at your church, you keep working on it. You focus on the larger goal beyond personal gain, and you construct a brighter future rather than simply secure the immediate relief. It takes an ongoing adjustment."

John nods and whispers, "That makes sense."

"Thanks, Wise-owl. Let's take Highway 19. But I'm not sure I will make it to see my dad with three more hours of driving."

"It's worth the safety for Fluffy." Wise-owl says, "I bet it will take more time to pass through this hostile city than to go the longer route. Can you imagine the hassle we'd have driving through a riot?

"Just think of it":

"Dog protestors are yanking the cats out of their boxes and hideouts. They are flipping over the police cars. It is turning ugly. All kinds of dogs are barking down Skinakat Lane. Hound dogs, bull dogs, and even hot dogs. It's a riot."

Road sign

They say a reasonable amount o' fleas is good for a dog–it keeps him from broodin' over bein' a dog mebble.

Edwards Noyes Westcott

Check Compass

Which one of the five responses do I use most often? Why? What one response I should start using more?

Act 3:

Cat Fight—Triaging Conflict.

Act 3: Scene 1: Managing Nerves.

The meowing and growling really gets on John's nerves.

"We should have gone through Dogsville and let them skin you alive." Buddy screams, not even five-hundred feet away from the on ramp to Dogsville.

"Would you two stop?" John says.

"Ever since you came" Buddy says, "John can't even sit with me for an hour without being busy chasing you around. You irresponsible jerk." With both paws he strikes out, straight to Fluffy's throat, as John takes a quick look in the mirror.

"Stop. Somebody is going to get hurt." John pulls over to the shoulder, takes out two leashes and chains Buddy and Fluffy at opposite corners of the backseat.

"You guys going to cool it or not?"

Sensing the tension between Buddy and Fluffy, Wise-owl hops back between them and say, "I know you both have reasons to feel hurt, fearful, or frustrated, and I don't blame you. Probably I would too if I were you. Can we talk about it?"

"Sure," says Buddy, and "Of course," says Fluffy.

"Wait," Wise-owl says, "let's take turns and . . ."

The conversation doesn't bother John, as he is already lost in his own world far away.

Wise-owl says, pointing to a road sign "Let's get a quick bite at the next exit. We're all hungry."

"I hope I'm doing the right thing." John whispers, turning to Wise-owl now that he is sitting next to him again.

"You are. You are compelling them to stop fighting, responding as a participant in the conflict. But you are also restraining them as a conflict manager."

John narrows his eyes, putting his slim finger across his lips, his usual gesture. "*Hmmmm.*"

"You choose one of the five ways of responding to conflict when you are directly involved, considering meeting your need and their need and the time you have. But if you are involved as a manager of the conflict, you can pick one of the three ways to handle it.

"The three ways are **return, restrain** and **resolve.** Your willingness and ability to handle the conflict and the intensity of the conflict will determine the method, and which of the three *Rs* you use. Let me show you."

Before Wise-owl finishes his sentence, he pulls out from his briefcase a long scroll.

"My teacher has given me this chart (adapted from Hugh F. Halverstadt's *Managing Church Conflict ©*). He said conflict is a drama without a script. Managing it is more an art than a science. Like courtship." The late Mrs. Owl was a wonderful lady. Wise-owl misses her.

"Once you are involved, your instinct and impulse will take you over the cliff, or your insight will guide you safely through the jungle.

"In the cool of the day, make sure to pre-wire yourself with this flow-chart before the heat of conflict flows. Be like the surgeons who set up knives, sponges and tubes; the 911 dispatchers who post their procedure; and the pilots who have their check lists."

Wise-owl unrolls a large diagram, full of colors, arrows and boxes.

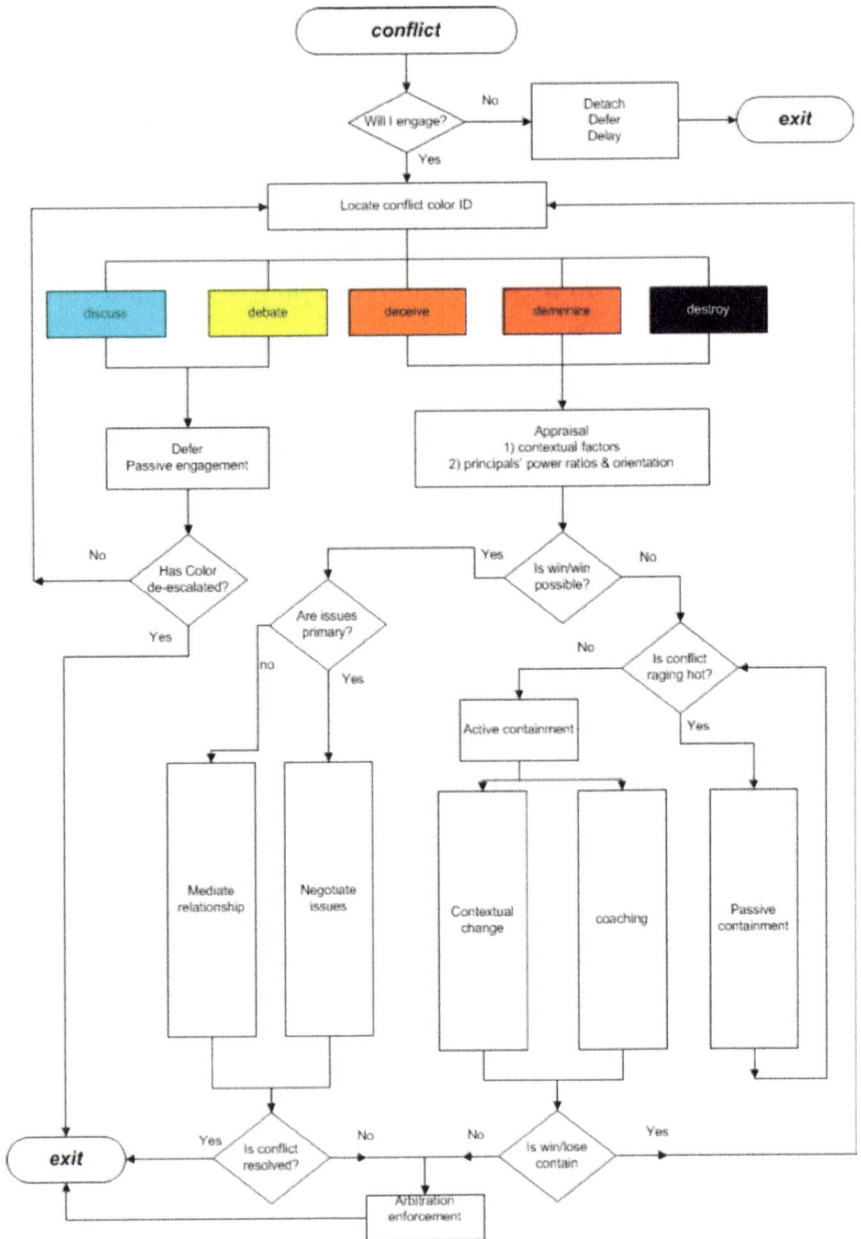

conflict

Will I engage? — No → Detach / Defer / Delay → exit

Yes

Locate conflict color ID

| discuss | debate | deceive | dethrone | destroy |

Defer
Passive engagement

Appraisal
1) contextual factors
2) principals' power ratios & orientation

Has Color de-escalated? — No / Yes

Is win/win possible? — Yes / No

Are issues primary? — no / Yes

Is conflict raging hot? — No / Yes

Active containment

Mediate relationship

Negotiate issues

Contextual change

coaching

Passive containment

Is conflict resolved? — Yes → exit / No

Arbitration enforcement

Is win/lose contain — No / Yes

Act 3: Scene 2: Using the Color ID.

John says, "I just saw the rest area sign three miles ahead. Let's stop there, so we can stretch and I can learn more."

By now, the dog and cat seem subdued because of the quick lunch, or being chained up, or because both have learned how to treat each other. John noticed a bit of weeping and hugging earlier. Three cheers for Wise-owl.

The rest area is clean, the air fresh, the sunshine warm. Perfect for a short break.

"It starts with a perceived conflict." Pointing to the chart, Wise-owl says, "In this case, you see Buddy and Fluffy fight like a dog and a cat. You decide to manage it because they are yours, and because we are all stuck together on this trip."

"So, I can't choose exit."

They both chuckle.

"That's right. We are stuck. But you can choose *return, restrain* or *resolve* depending on the level of your involvement as a manager and the intensity of the conflict between the players."

"I have just chained them up. Is that *restrain*?"

"Yes, that's *restrain*. When things are out of control and you put a container around it. Think of a choke-hold to someone's neck in a fight, or a restraining order in a domestic violence situation. In the chart, *out of control* refers to a hot conflict that needs a barricade, a box, a container."

Wise-owl points to the diamond-shaped box on the right side of the chart. He drags his paws gently across the words *Is conflict raging hot.*

"Usually, the orange, red, and black zones will need either *restrain* or *resolve,* depending upon the temperature of the conflict. For sure, you exercise *restrain* when it is too hot.

"When it is cool enough to talk and think, you choose *resolve.* You can often select *return* in the blue and yellow zone."

"What do all these colors mean?" John asks, directing his fingers to the chart.

"That's what we call the ***Color ID. Color Identification.*** It is a triage tool. The different colors tell you the different intensity of conflicts. The situation gets more serious as it moves from blue to yellow, orange, red and black; changes from discuss to debate, deceive, demonize, and destroy." Wise-owl waves his wings towards Buddy and Fluffy chained up across the parking lot.

No major response. Just a slight movement of their heads.

John is getting it, but eager to learn more. He likes a steady diet of information.

Wise-owl continues. "The fighter's goal and language often reveal the intensity of the fight. Some use numbers to grade the level, like the Richter scale of an earthquake. My teacher has chosen color to name the nature and seriousness of the conflict. Let's pull out the Color ID for you."

Wise-owl removes a big book mark from his pocket. "It's rather self-explanatory. Why don't you take a minute to read it and ask me questions then?"

The Color ID Chart

	Nature	Goal	Language	Dynamic	Intervention
Blue	Discuss	Solve problem	Specific and clear	Rational	At lowest level. Tasks mutual
Yellow	Disagree	Self-protect	General & emotional	Triangulation starts. "We don't have good communication here"	At highest level, task mutual. Express feelings publicly
Orange	Deceive	Win	Distorted, exaggerated, "right" vs. "wrong"	Emotion over fact, coalition form, assume intention & motive	At highest level. Task mutual, set rules. Negotiate, search for larger goal
Red	Demonize	Hurt	Ideological	Faction with a leader, signal "We're in the fight." From issue to principle	Need outside help, work with leader. Safeguard rules, personal rights, and procedure.
Black	Destroy	Eradicate	Destructive	Ends over means	Use peace keeping force

"When Buddy and Fluffy fight, they are in the red zone right?" John asks.

"Yes. They are getting physical. They want to hurt each other. Buddy demonizes Fluffy as the cause of your inattentiveness. His language is more than exaggerated, and they need outside help."

"Will they remain in the red zone for long?"

"Hopefully not. The color will change as the fight escalates or de-escalates. Conflict is not a single event, but an emotional process where truth has different meanings to different people. It changes constantly.

"If you kick a pebble, the pebble will be thrown as a projectile, according to physics. The action has physical cause and effect without any meaning involved. But when you kick a dog, that pooch will return the favor or run away, according to what's goes on in his mind, depending if he's a Pit Bull or a Chihuahua.

"Nobel Prize winning writer Czeslaw Milosz said, 'My past changes every minute according to the meaning given it now, in the moment.'

"Our job is to decode the meaning and to de-escalate the conflict. Remember the Wind talkers in WWII? They spoke Navajo so the enemies couldn't get to the message. Your goal is to decode that coded message." John tries to catch up after a short mental detour as Wise-owl continues.

"Please remember, the combatants can be in different zones at the same times. Fluffy may be in the yellow zone when Buddy is in the red. In other words, someone can be very mad at you, but you are completely unaware of it.

A conflict can move along. The focus usually starts with the issue, "you owe me money", then moves to others, "you are such a jerk" and then turns toward self alone, "He makes me so mad. How can I get even?"

You try to intervene with the one at the darkest color zone."

"What about the 3Rs; the *return*, *restrain* and *resolve*?" John asks, pointing to the chart.

"Great! You've given me an idea." With that, Wise-owl writes on a piece of paper these words.

Conflict is inevitable
Needs determine fit
Triage and the 3Rs.

Act 3: Scene 3: Lessons from the Monkey.

'**ve** just touched on **restrain** a bit, but before I fill in more details, let's start from the beginning.

The first R is **Return**. It means *you* are not going to manage the problem. You will return the problem to the primary players in the conflict. You can do it in three ways. **Detach, Deflect** and **Delay**. Detach is the maximum disengagement. Literally wash your hand off the matter. Can you think of any example?"

"Oh yes," says John. "I remember a fight at our feeding site for the homeless. It was too much for us to handle, so I called the police. I didn't do anything except fill out the police report.

"Usually the people are pretty well behaved, and they police themselves. That day a fight seemed to have already been brewing, as people had issues with one other outside the building before this incident."

"Good," says Wise-owl. "You made the right choice. Let's move to the next level from *detach* to *deflect*. It means re-routing the conflict to the sender. In other words, when people give you the monkey, don't accept it, give them back the monkey. Again, any example?"

"I think the kids at church often fight over who 'did' and who 'did not!' Whenever Tom and Jerry get together, they make trouble. Tom will say, 'he kicked me,' and Jerry will say, 'he kicked me first,' and so on and on. I just can't figure out who is telling the truth. How do I return the monkey?"

"Remember, you are not an eye witness or an inspector of the crime. All you see is a snapshot. For ***return*** to work, you need to focus on the temporary solution. Tell them to take turns asking "What do you want me to do" and "What don't you want me to do." That is a good way to help them settle minor disputes on their own.

"The adult version is, 'this doesn't seem to be working for either of us. It is not working for me because— What would work better for me is—Would that work for you?'

"Or you can get semi-involved and help them role-play a likely upcoming scenario. You can sit in as a mediator, or walk away and let them follow up with questions and answers."

"I will do this with Tom and Jerry next time. Now, what about *delay*?"

"You use *delay* when the timing, the circumstances, or the people are not quite ready to settle things. Do you remember any incident like that?"

Without hesitation, John tells of the unfair, untrue, and mocking remark Maria hurled at him at a birthday party when he greeted her with a handshake. "Well, you finally talk to me." She said it loudly, right within earshot of the crowd by the punch bowl. She glared up from her wheelchair, head tilted, lips tight, and on her face a smirk.

"Where did this come from? He had just visited her and helped her to the hospital a few times last month. He could have corrected her, but he is the pastor who supposed to be good and godly. He stumbled for a response and didn't say much. But he was fuming inside. His heart cried foul."

"That's a sniper attack." Wise-owl says. A cheap shot, knowing you will not respond because it would escalate into a long- drawn-out verbal combat in public, which you dread. You were in the firing range. She took cover in her hide-out of illness and irritability.

"Snipers hate exposure.

"One thing you can do to expose a sniper without being dragged into an argument is to say something like this: 'Maria, I am sorry you feel that way, and I feel something entirely different. Let's talk about it later when we have more time.'

"Talk about delay, let's check on Buddy and Fluffy."

Turning towards John's Sienna mini-van, they both notice a spooky glowing hue across Mt. Humongus.

Act 3: Scene 4: Getting a Grip on R. R. R.

The glow doesn't radiate the beauty and tenderness of the setting sun, but the harshness of a blazing trail set by dragons spitting fire near the foothills. Ghostly smoke is climbing up, trying to capture the mountain top.

They must have talked for a long time while the sun began to set to not have noticed such an eerie monster lighting up the fading mountain. As they pass around the bend, it dawns on them that this must be the hill fire as seen on TV just before they left Securatown.

"This fire gives us a perfect example of a *restrain*," Wise-owl says, as they all return to the Sienna and buckle up.

The 3 Rs.
1. Return. 2. Restrain. 3. Resolve

"We have talked about **return**. Now let's go on to **restrain**. In Securatown, we had heard that the fire was seventy-five percent contained, in other words, restrained.

"You have just restrained the dog and cat with leashes, right?"

Wise-owl doesn't wait for the answer.

"Restrain is the strategy and containment is the tool. When the fire is raging mad, the first goal is to restrain it from spreading. The medic calls it, 'first do no harm.'

"So, bringing on the hoses is just a way to cool it down, not to put it out. Instead, the firemen watch the direction of the wind and dig ditches to build the containment.

"Likewise, to contain an earthquake, a storm, or a flood, you board houses, tie down boats, and sandbag the coastline. You can think of a million examples."

"How's that apply to conflict?" John asks.

"Next time when you see two people throwing fists at each other, do you try to resolve it by asking them to 'calm down' and reason together, or do you try to turn the monkey back and say go ahead and fight it out. Or do you restrain them physically first and reason later?"

"Separate them first, of course; they are out of control."

"That's right," Wise-owl says. "Like the raging fire, hot conflict by definition is out of control, chaotic, and often unpredictable. All want to have the upper hand, to dominate and to control the situation. Truth means nothing. Winning means everything. So, they fight. But fight only invites fighting back.

"Either one of them backs out (*self-restrained*) or someone has to hold them down. It takes a cool head and a strong ego to restrain ourselves.

"Internal restraint allows us to absorb emotional encounters without having to have an obvious reaction to them. The point isn't to deny the feelings or bottle them up, but to hold them in check. Recognize the emotion but don't be emotional.

"Martin Luther King, Jr. and Gandhi are great examples."

Instead of thinking how good self-restraint is, John is going the opposite direction in his mental monologue.

"I have far too much of this self-restraint stuff, biting my tongue when I shouldn't." He recounts incident upon incident when he should have confronted the wrong and felt better about himself, but he didn't. He is too nice. Or is he?

He should have forbidden the small group meetings when they started inviting guest speakers whose theology had not been checked, but he had wanted to give them the benefit of the doubt.

He should have stopped the gossip of one group against another. But he didn't want to end up offending both.

He should have . . .

"I need to start all over."

In the middle of John's resolution, Wise-owl chimes in.

"By the way, don't say 'calm down' when people are mad." Wise-owl says, "It only makes them madder. Well, we're all hungry. Can we try to find a place for dinner?

"While you drive, I can read you something my teacher has written about restrain and containment. You can ask me more questions when we take a break, *okay?*"

Wise-owl takes out some papers, browses through them, and starts reading. John holds on to the steering wheel with both hands closed and both ears open:

Strategy of containment.

"John, I am defining this in reference to the flow chart and using some of my own words, *okay?*" He continues to read, with his claws tracking the words and arrows on the wrinkled scroll.

Passive containment. "Is the conflict raging hot or chaotic? If yes, then use *passive containment,* like calling a break, ending a phone call, or refusing to interact. First, do no harm, and next, draw a line around the chaos.

"You stop the destructive behavior and prevent the exchange by putting a choke hold on the situation. You wait passively for the fuel to burn itself up, so that order can emerge from the chaos."

Assessing the peaceful backseat meeting Buddy and Fluffy are now in, Wise-owl feels he can continue reading.

"You can contain conflict not by direct confrontation or even persuasion and reasoning, but by setting up barriers and using the collective power of the bystanders. Examples of containment include the no-fly-zone, county jail, and the courthouse. UN peacekeeping force, the prison guards, and judges are the bystanders.

"It takes time to cool the emotional heat down and then move from the fight and survival instinct to a more sober judgment, and even to a resolution."

Wise-owl stops for a moment, looks at John and says, "You know, in some ways, the surveillance camera is a powerful passive container. You know why?"

"I guess when people know they are being watched and videotaped they will be less inclined to do the wrong thing.

It is like being barricaded by a wall of public judgment. They will behave better in front of the camera."

Affirming John's conclusion, Wise-owl says, "Right. Like a hurricane heading onshore. The wind cannot sustain its destructive course and peters out when it gets past the coast. The land defeats the storm just by being there."

"Come to think about it," John says, after a quick search in his mental files, "As I watched the Occupy Movement a while back, gearing up in LA for a mid-night showdown with the police, I noticed something. Both the police and the occupiers were taking videos of the arrests.

"An hour or two earlier, before the police cascaded down the steps of city hall with a massive show of force; they already had set up parameters along many city blocks to contain the possible riot. Only after that did they start arresting those who resisted leaving.

"Both sides were taking close-up videos and several city blocks were secured. Everyone was relieved when it ended rather peacefully with only a few arrests. I think the video camera is providing an effective, passive, but not obvious restraint."

"Great insight." Wise-owl nods.

Wise-owl reads on.

"***Active containment*** uses tools like coaching and changing the context to reorient the combatants to fight constructively before the real resolution begins.

"We do that after the conflict cools down to a manageable level and after we use passive containment. We move from the black and red zone to the orange and blue or yellow zone.

"Coaching means spending private time with the combatants to help them identify how fair or dirty they are fighting and give them some tips on how to fight fair. You want to equip them with some good resolution skills.

"A lot of people don't have the skill to reduce the occasions of conflict, or to deescalate or resolve it when it happens."

John continues driving, and Buddy and Fluffy are tuning in to the conversation also. They are all ears.

"Contextual change means changing the rules and context of the interaction, like changing the decision-making process to make sure each person's idea counts fairly, meeting in a neutral place, doing anything to level the playing field. I think King Arthur started the round table to do just that.

"Power, though largely contextual and relative, is the currency in negotiating a conflict. To level the playing field is to give all the players an equal footing on the power base. People tend to fight dirty if they feel powerless.

"Other rules are: no hearsay, state the facts and feelings only from a personal account, or from accounts of two or more eye- witnesses, no name calling, and no guessing of others' intentions. Besides these, agree on rules of behavior, and mutually craft a vision statement for a desirable solution.

"Sometimes, just asking, 'after this is settled, what will be an ideal outcome look like to you?' will establish a sense of direction. An answer gives hope and unites the combatants in setting the course for problem solving.

"Furthermore, reframe the conflict into a dispute, and then break up the dispute into different issues, creating a final goal line. This will put a complex conflict into something linear, something smaller and manageable, so that the conflict will not have a life of its own.

"At the heart of conflict is really the struggle to dominate. The fighter doesn't care about the issue, only about winning and defeating the enemy. *Disputes* are often symptoms of an underlying conflict which might be resolved once the dispute is settled, but often it can't be.

"Because a lawsuit contains a conflict as a dispute, many times even the conclusion of a lawsuit does not resolve the underlying conflict in any real way. The legal process is structurally unable to deal with our souls, with the issues of intolerance, love, forgiveness, and vengeance."

Wise-owl stops to breathe, and asks "Are you ready for third R?"

"Of course."

"*Strategy for Resolution*: After the temperature cools down enough, we can start to resolve the problem, particularly with coaching. First question asked is '*Are issues primary*?' If *yes*, then we identify and name the problems and set goals. Next, we can generate solutions through open dialogue, fact finding, brainstorming, or mind-mapping.

"The critical thing to remember at this stage is to move from the stated positions to the underlining interest— e.g. 'I hear you say what your position is. You're not going to drive. But it sounds to me as if what you really want out of this is a van that runs safely.

"*Position* locks us in a contest. *Interest* leads us to problem solving.

"*Mediate relationship* is the strategy used to enhance peoples' ability to deal with relational difficulties. Here are some tips.

"Address their disrupted relationship in specific behavioral terms instead of emotional content, and restate accusations of bad intentions into the impact you have felt upon you."

"Wait, Wise-owl. What do you mean?"

"Say something like, 'I don't know whether you intended to embarrass me in public, but I felt very uncomfortable when you did so-and-so.' Now you are not judging or accusing him, but simply stating the impact upon you.

"Instead of saying, 'I know you want to hurt me' say, 'I was hurt when you did so-and-so.'

"Instead of saying, 'You don't care,' say something specific. Cite the behavior that shows what you don't care looks like, 'When you don't look at me when I talk to you, I feel you don't care.'

"Also, saying, 'Help me understand where you are coming from on this.'

"Ask each combatant to take turns and tell their story of a few critical incidents they have found destructive to their relationship. Set ground rules such as no name calling, no second-guessing of intentions, state the blame in terms of mutual contributions to the problem.

"The goal is to look at the relational conflict from different angles, clear the air, and vent emotions.

"While *negotiating issues* encourages emotional self-control, *mediating relationships* asks for emotional expression. Notice even when the relationship takes center stage, if it is too messy, negotiating the issue comes first. Sometimes it is easier, less embarrassing, and less risky to admit to a substantive problem than to a relational problem.

"Often, we have to pursue these two strategies side by side. It all depends on the circumstances.

"This is critical at this stage to ask questions. Ask how each person sees things.

"You can say, 'my sense is that you and I see this situation differently; I would like to share how I'm seeing it, and learn more about how you're seeing it.'

Wise-owl stops reading for a moment, looks up, and says, "Ask a lot of question. Ask for meanings beyond facts, impact rather than intention, and contribution rather than blame. Douglas Stone, Sheila Heen, and Bruce Patton, of The Harvard Negotiation Project have written a wonderful book called *Difficult Conversations* ©. Everyone should read it."

"What are some of the questions you should ask?" John asks.

"It depends, but here are some very useful ones."

With pen and paper, Wise-owl scribbles across the page:

My top ten questions

- How do you feel about it?
- What do you think about it?
- Can you please help me understand . . . ?
- Can you tell me more?
- Where do I go wrong if I say . . . ?
- What do you see as an area of common ground or interest?
- What is it that you need from each other?
- What are you hearing him/her say?
- What led you to believe he/she doesn't trust you?
- Most people lose something in conflict. What are you losing?

John is listening with his heart and eyes wide open, but all their stomachs are shrinking and growling. What a great relief to see the 5 Miles Ahead sign of the Golden Arches.

"I am sure you have questions. This is just a condensed version of dealing with conflict after the triage.

"*Return* when you don't want to get involved. *Restrain* when the temperature is sizzling. *Resolve* when the parties are ready to find a solution. We will discuss more on resolve later."

"The chart certainly helps, and your ten favorite questions are handy," John says.

"But that's not enough. You must apply CPR," Wise-owl says.

"What's that?" John asks.

"Tell you later."

From the back seat Buddy and Fluffy both sing in unison, "Are we there yet?"

Road Sign

Listening allows change to take place without forcing it.

Check Compass

Looking back at some relationships, which was the worst and why?

How would you manage it differently?

Act 4:

Motel CPR—Decoding the DNA of Conflict.

Act 4: Scene 1: Enter the Stretcher.

Big Mac comforts the stomachs, but not as much as the motel bed that soothes the soul and warms the feet. They all need the break and rest. Somehow John senses CPR is coming.

The night is cool and quiet, the dog and cat are warm and asleep, and Wise-owl is settling in his lotus position next to the nightstand.

John is in his pajamas, but he can't sleep. He combs his fingers through his hair. He recalls what he has just learned.

Conflict is natural. He can be planting a seed for good or evil by the way he handles it. The common responses are *compel, avoid, negotiate, accommodate* or *collaborate,* based upon meeting his need vs. others' need, and the amount of time available to deal with the problem.

He has also learned how to use Color ID to triage the intensity of the conflict, by observing the parties' goals and language. Judging from how hot the conflict is, he can manage it with *Return*, *Restrain* or *Resolve*.

Will these tools be enough to prepare him to see his dad, his uncle Robert, and his family? What about facing up to himself—who he is, and how he wants to be the nicest and the only fire hydrant in Dogsville.

Looking back, his people's secret meetings, anonymous letters to the bishop demanding his head, and all the spitefulness towards his children deeply hurt and puzzle him.

John didn't even know he was in the hot seat until the bishop called him. But why?

What about his uneasiness in dealing with conflict, in standing up for himself or for what is right? Why is he so timid?

Why are people sometimes so unkind and unreasonable?

Why are the people who were so nice at the welcome meeting the same people who now want to destroy him? What has brought about such a drastic change?

Why can't they tell him directly what's wrong?

Why can't Buddy and Fluffy get along?

Why did his uncle so despise him as a young boy, and sneer at his family all these years?

Will what Wise-owl has just said, "You must apply CPR" give him the answer?

Act 4: Scene 2: CPR to the Rescue.

"John, why don't you sleep? Thinking about CPR? In my duffle bag over there, you will find my teacher's article on that subject. If that can make you feel better, go ahead and read it and get some sleep.

"Before you read it, remind yourself that conflict becomes difficult to manage when people direct all their attention at one another, rather than at the dynamic that holds them hostage to their hostility. CPR will unlock the secret of that dynamic."

By now, John is sweating over these puzzles in his head. He can't resist and heads for Wise-owl's bag.

Fortunately, the few pages seem short. He slips into bed.

"Conflict is an evolving drama of reciprocal functioning between three parts of conflict: the *Conflict, the Players and the Roadmap. CPR.*

Let's start with the most obvious matter first: the *conflict*, the declared problem, the issue at hand, the fight itself. The *C*.

The Conflict (C): Church fights are rarely about what is right and wrong, but about the lack of appreciation and respect, or acknowledgement of the differences. The role and performance of the pastors, the congregational size changes, and the mission of the church are the focus of most of the fights.

"His sermon is lousy, more like a Bible Study than worship" "Why do we need another service when our Sunday morning is not full?"

"We may as well burn the song books if all we do is look at the screen."

As long as a fight remains in the blue and yellow zone, it is a fair fight. But once the intent is to hurt and defame, to attack the motive and legitimacy of the individuals, or to threaten to quit if we can't get our way, the fight gets dirty fast.

Within the fight are problems to *solve*, or problems to *manage*. Problems to solve are often substantive (involving resources or things), systemic (unclear or overlapping structure, e.g. ill-defined job descriptions), or informational (different parties have different parts of the information).

Except for problems that are psychological or demonic, usually there is a solution, if you look long enough.

Problems to manage are those problems that cannot be solved. The most common are conflicts revolving around polarities and values.

Value conflicts (pro-life vs. pro-choice) may have solutions, imperfect that they may be, but peoples' commitments to certain priorities, goals, and methods are so deeply ingrained in their characters or identities that to change one's value is next to impossible. So, agree to disagree.

Polarity conflicts refers to interdependent opposites (e.g. the need to inhale and exhale). Seemingly these are two opposite poles, but you need them both. When you do one, you create the need of the other. Discipleship or evangelism? Work or faith? Centralization or decentralization? Personal privacy or national security? Is wire-tap justified in the aftermath of 9/11?

Usually we get trapped in the self-imposed limitation of either/ or thinking—insisting the downside of the present pole is the problem, and the upside of the other pole is the only solution.

Polarity runs its course on a pendulum. Insisting that the opposite or the current pole is the only right answer will invite problems as the pendulum swings the other way. Try inhaling without exhaling. So, monitor the pendulum.

Understand the two necessary opposites with their ups and downs, and balance the need of the two extremes.

Manage the problem by getting the benefit of each side, while appreciating their limits.

John can hear the dog snores and the cat sneeze.

The Players (P): The players are the people involved in the conflict, the bystanders and the manager. Their belief about themselves, good and evil, the nature of conflict, and their learned skills in response to anxiety, fear, anger, and their ability to self-differentiate will largely determine how they will handle the conflict.

Belief drives all conflict, but feelings of shame, powerlessness, and fear almost always create a dirty fight. The deadliest stance is self-righteousness. Morality asks what is right. Self-righteousness declares, "You are wrong." When people are fueled with passion, any means to get revenge is justified.

So, in the name of God and to get rid of the infidel, terrorists blew up the twin towers. In the name of church survival, well- intentioned dragons spit fire upon those evildoers who "NEVER have an altar call, NEVER preach about sin, and ALWAYS play that loud ungodly music."

John can't resist, but enters into another world vivid with sight, sound and sorrow.

"Pastor John, let me talk to you," Daryl said, closing his door with a gentle slam, a funereal look, and a slow walk to John's uncluttered desk. Putting aside his cane as he sat down, he said, wasting no time "Why don't you tell those people to stop talking in the chapel? The chapel is a holy place. And why don't you ever preach about sin?"

Ever? It has been only three months since he arrived at The First Securatownian Church. These guys are so legalistic and so hostile towards visitors. They say they are a friendly church, but friendly to whom?

What are they afraid of? Why do they bark at visitors? Is that self-righteousness or what? Is Daryl a well-intentioned dragon?

I preach the same sermon every Sunday morning at Summer Breeze RV Park before coming to Securatownian. They give me a warm welcome, they like my sermon, but here they spit at me, they hate what others like. Why is that?

Back to the reading.

Conflict also means 'an anxious situation unresolved.' Not all anxiety is bad. Crisis generates acute anxiety. Our reptilian brain responds quickly and instinctively to threat. We fight, we freeze, or we flee in self-defense for our survival.

Chronic anxiety is habitual. How badly we see ourselves and the world takes root in our psyche. With little capacity to discern between the acute and the chronic, plus a low tolerance for pain and a highly reactive emotional makeup, the chronically anxious person will reduce every reaction to all or nothing.

He or she will conduct a search-and-destroy mission to secure immediate relief in stressful situations. Or they will quit with a complete, no middle of the ground, disengagement.

Another way they may control anxiety is through the process of triangulation, and gossip is a common form of triangulation. Simply put, two people talk about the third person or situation. Quite often it is a way to get rid of anguish instead of dealing with it.

Gossip triangles two people on the inside as gossipers and a third person on the outside as a burden-bearer. The burden is the load the gossipers are not comfortable dealing with directly.

Shifting the burden, however, does not lift it. It only relocates it. Pastors, because of their position of responsibility and vulnerability, are often the object of triangling.

John can't help but think about the parking-lot blabbermouths talking about Daryl when they should have talked directly with him.

John can't help but think of Buddy and Fluffy when they come to complain about each other to him. They want to triangle him into the situation.

John can't help but think about the women groups' underground dart-throwing meetings, with him at the center of the dart board. They should talk to him face to face, but throwing darts is easier in his absence.

Hmmmm. That's triangulation. He reads on.

Habitually anxious people often lack self-differentiation, the healthy response to the balance between the need to be a separate unique individual and the need to connect with others in a community.

Community means that two or more unique people meet together for relationships. Fuzzy individuals merge, fuse, or stick together in a *collective*.

However, when we are anxious, we are more instinctive than insightful. Without the ability to self-differentiate and draw boundaries, the anxious persons are pulled toward one of the extremes—emotional distance, or emotional fusion.

When fusers fail to establish a relationship, they quit. They exchange one extreme for the other. If John compared the list of those who welcomed him into the new church and those who want to get rid of him, he would be amazed at the overlap.

The line is thin between deifying and crucifying John, between putting him on a pedestal and trashing him in the dumpster.

Wasn't it Daryl and his gang who were so gung ho to welcome him in the beginning, but now, in just three months grilled him. Daryl lost his job shortly after John arrived. Was it part of the reason for his anxiety?

Perhaps he wanted to fuse with him, but John has his own life and is just trying to settle in. Daryl is only one of many in the church John needs to care for. Is this why the vicious attack?

Is this why his predecessor is still glued to these people, contacting them often, filling his own need to be needed?

Flipping the page, just one left, John continues reading:

*The Roadmap (R)***:** This is the most inconspicuous part of the conflict, yet it often leads us to trouble. *Roadmap* refers to the relationship, the framework, the connection between the players, the conflict, and the situation. A bad roadmap is the problematic situation, context, system or structure (organizational or family) in which conflict often is created, sustained, and resolved.

Conflict travels along the relational and systemic pathway. People who engage in conflict are not necessarily bad people, but in a bad situation. They have a bad roadmap.

Wise-owl says, "The saying 'If you hang around the barber shop, you will get a haircut soon.' applies to the understanding of conflict."

"What do you mean by that?" John asks.

"Look at it this way, if you give people a bigger plate, they will eat more. If you hang out with the baseball pitcher, sooner or later you will chew and spit. If you put a good person in a lousy system, the system often wins. *System* can produce conflict.

"People risk getting a ticket to park in the no-parking zone at LAX to pick up friends and family. Lawbreaker? Inconsiderate? Or may be parking is impossible. A great solution is to designate a Cell phone waiting area. If we look long enough, we can provide a better roadmap.

"You see, the same roadmap is there when parents pick up little kids from school. People double park or park on red curbs and next to fire-hydrants. Bad roadmap wins. Good people lose.

"In church organizational system, *roadmap* refers to the rules, roles, and goals: formal, informal, and tacit. These systems behave as if they are persons. They act to preserve themselves, resist changes, and maneuver people into roles and expectations to maintain the status quo and balance. This system's dynamic is called 'homeostatic.'

For example, our formal goal, written or conscious, declares Youth Outreach a priority, but the informal goal, conscious, unwritten, nudges us to sustain adult membership, and the tacit goal, unwritten, unspoken, warns us quietly to grease the hierarchy.

"Anyone in such a system will see the folly, feel the double bind, but hide the hypocrisy to survive the system.

"Everything will be fine for a while. Conflict comes when we upset the apple cart, rock the boat, test the assumption, or declare that the emperor has no clothes.

"Here is the chart to show a church roadmap leading to conflict.

Roadmap of First Securatownian Church

	Rule	Role	Goal
Formal	Recognize Mother's Day at worship	Pastor	Grow Sunday School
Informal	Take ladies out to lunch	Problem solver	Take care of senior members
tacit	Buy them lunch and give them flowers	provider	Keep general statistics up

"We often don't know the informal rule and the tacit rule until we break it. I broke some of those: 'Take your ladies out for lunch and bring them flowers on Mother's Day.' I started a fight without knowing it. I brought them flowers but didn't treat them lunch. Knowing the history of a church is crucial.

"Have you been in an elevator full of strangers? Try asking them some very personal questions and see what happens. Lesson? Open your eyes and ears before your mouth. Understand the roadmap.

"Wow," says John. "this is so true of Securitownian Church. The roadmap is full of landmines."

John's eyes are getting heavy and his head is getting light. "CPR, conflict, people, roadmap. *Ah*, my church, so dysfunctional, so co-dependent, so pharisaical. They want a manager, not a leader. They want a clock, not a compass. No wonder they need a pastor who needs to be needed. Oh well.

The strings of events are swimming across his heavy eyelids. He is gaining some clarity into what he is dealing with and who he is.

Are we there yet?

Road Sign

The diamond cannot be polished without friction, nor the man perfected without trials.

Chinese Proverbs

Check Compass

What is one insight I have gained in CPR that I can use now?

What one thing I can do to make a better roadmap?

Act 5:

Cowpalace—Managing Conflict:

Act 5: Scene 1: Close but Far

John doesn't go easy on the gas pedal, hoping to blast through the thirty miles to Cowpalace, the home of the Mad Cow, Sacred Cow, Beefy Cow, Regular Cow, Milky Cow, and Holy Cow; gateway to John's hometown, the Everland.

However, the new gateway to John's present church conflict and yesteryear's family feud is conflict resolution. He needs more than what he'd just learned.

"Are we there yet?" Buddy and Fluffy say in perfect harmony. "Yes, soon. About thirty minutes to the terminal and another half an hour for the ferry ride."

John is eager to see his dad. Now he knows much more about conflict than he did two days ago. Perhaps he knows a little more about himself.

He knows how to define, triage, return, and restrain conflict, but to resolve it is still another story. He wants to know.

He needs to know. He is going to see his family in just a few hours. How he wishes to rush over and line up for the ferry.

Oh, mercy, he is going to cross the ferry soon, he assumes.

But it doesn't turn out that way.

Instead of long lines of cars and trucks waiting for the boat, the lot is filled with two-legged and four-legged creatures holding up sticks and signs. Next to the huge billboards "Ferry Closed" "You get, we sweat" "Get the dogs out" parade dozens of cow policemen and picketers. Some bystanders and reporters are busy talking and taking pictures.

Horrified, John goes over to the ferry terminal to find out what is going on.

"The union is on strike demanding a better ramp, better health plan, better pay, and better ferry safety. Everyone except Sacred Cow is also complaining about the ferry system, as long as Cowpalace refuses to build a bridge."

John's heart skips a beat.

"Wise-owl, the cows are mad and the ferry's not running. I'm going to miss my dad."

Agonizing silence lasts a few seconds, though it seems hours.

"If you will write a letter, I can fly over and read it to him. He can hear me even in a coma."

"*Okay*. Would you watch Buddy and Fluffy? I'll go over to the rest area."

In no time, words planned long ago are flowing across his notepad.

> Dear dad. It's John. I came right away, but the ferry is not running. Please forgive me for not seeing you more often.
>
> It has been twenty-five years since I left home in anger. I know you cared and you loved us, but you just didn't know how to show it. Having Sarah now helps me understand you better. We all have regrets and have done wrong. Before mom died, she told me she had forgiven you. Me too. Please forgive me.
>
> Poverty has taken a toll on us and driven you to gambling. Perhaps we should talk more. Perhaps . . . but that's not important any more. You are my dad and I love you.

There is something I want to tell you, and should have done it long time ago.

I couldn't find peace in my heart for many years, carrying a lot of resentment, working two jobs while going to college. I was angry at you and myself, until my Chemistry professor introduced me to Christ.

He told me I can find peace when I know the Prince of Peace, Jesus Christ. He will forgive me when I ask. I could not believe how one person born so long ago can forgive my sin. What sin? Then he told me this story:

On a cold snowy night, Norm was reading his book by the fireplace. He heard pecking noises by the window and realized a bird was trying to get in.

He thought, "This bird is going to freeze to death soon. If I open the window, I will scare him away. If I don't, he will die. How can I get him inside the house?"

After some thinking, he came up with an idea. If he can *become* a bird he can fly out to the backyard, meet the bird, talk with him and lead him inside the house through the back door. So Norm became a bird because he wanted to reach out to a bird.

The bird was saved.

My Chemistry professor then read to me from his Bible, John 1:1 and 1:14 'In the beginning was the Word, and the Word was with God, and the Word was God.

And the Word became flesh, and made his dwelling among us. We have seen His glory, the glory of the One and Only, who came from the Father, full of grace and truth.'

He said, "If God wanted to reach out to a dog, he would become a dog. Since he wanted to reach out to humans, he became a human. You know, religion is man reaching out to God; Christianity is God reaching out to man."

I asked, "Is there a God?"

"How can there be a photo without a photographer, a painting without a painter, a watch without a watch maker, a building without a builder, creatures without a creator?"

"Abraham Lincoln said, 'I can see how it might be possible for a man to look down upon the earth and be an atheist, but I cannot conceive how he could look up into the heavens and say there is no God.'"

He reasoned with me from the complexity of creation, the words of the Bible, the historical Jesus, his perfect moral teachings and his miracles. I was convinced.

The empty tomb gave the invincible proof.

That long dialogue and the bird story made my heart tender and tumbled my long-standing religious misconception castle. I gave my life to Jesus Christ.

I found peace and forgiveness from the one who makes me. That's why years later I became a pastor, though I have a civil engineer job waiting for me.

I am not perfect nor without problems, but life has taken on a new meaning and perspective. I can see things I couldn't see, as a caterpillar turns into a butterfly. Dad, I really want you to know Jesus Christ too. Forgive me for not telling you until now.

I wish and pray the ferry will run soon. I love you, dad.

Your son, John.

John races toward the car with letter in hand. Halfway across the parking lot, he hears someone shouting, "John, come quickly, they are talking about the ferry on the radio."

Act 5: Scene 2: The Billy Goat's Mediation

Shortly after Wise-owl disappears into the blue sky toward Everland, John glues himself to the radio. Buddy and Fluffy are equally cemented.

Bang! Bang! Bang! Sounds of that gavel call for attention.

"Fellow cows, this is Moo from KCOW 9 Channel Cowpalace, reporting inside Cow City Chamber. All kind of cows are packing the room wall to wall. Tempers are flaring. The mayor is calling the meeting to order.

"I am waiting for the protestors to make their case. Cow police are passing a microphone to one of them.

"Mr. Mayor, my name is Sacred Cow. We founded Cowpalace. When we first settled here there was hardly anything, until we began building large boats to connect us with Everland. Now, Holy Cow wants to build a bridge and destroy the peace and our way of life. We need to support and subsidize the ferry system, not to demolish it!"

A resounding mix of cheers and jeers follows.

Holy Cow says, "My real name is Mad Cow. I am not trying to destroy our way of life, but to make it better. I have seen how they abused Beefy cows who build and run the ferry. So Beefy formed the union to fight off Sacred Cow.

The Union and the Ferry didn't get along either and strikes were frequent. Finally I came up with the idea of building bridges. After that, every time I speak, they mock me, saying,

"Holy Cow!" Since then, I have founded the Holy Cow Association.

Roar, roar, roar. Gavel, gavel, gavel.

"Order please!" says the mayor. "The conflict here is hurting our city, our future and our cowlowship. In a few years, Cowpalace will be a ghost town. Even now, most people don't know this little town exists. People just drive by to the next attraction."

Few boos, some moans, but most remain silent.

"I have invited Billy Goat from Billyland to mediate our dispute. He is a peacemaker well known among cows, goats, and pigs. Mr. Goat, would you please begin?"

Billy Goat says, "No doubt we have some strong differences, and I trust that we are all here in good faith striving to resolve the problem. The alternative is to fight, strike, and have a dying town. Our discussion will not to get rid of disagreements and secure victory, but make progress.

I would like to do three things, and first, here are some ground rules: no name calling, no hearsay, and take turns to talk without interruption. Agreed?

"Agreed."

"We will do the following: *Explain the Conflict*, *Extract the Concerns*, and *Explore the Conclusion*. Let's write it on the board for you. Mr. Bark, would you read it out loud for the benefit of those listening on the radio and those at the back of the room?"

The city clerk starts putting large letters on the huge white chalkboard. Moo reports:

Resolving conflict in 3 EC ways
Explain Conflict
Extract Concern
Explore Conclusion

"First, from your point of view, explain what you see as the conflict. Sacred Cow, could you start?"

Sacred Cow is fed up with all the 'Paradigm stuff' from Holy Cow. Nobody appreciates his building the city from the ground up. Holy Cow's idea of constructing a bridge will certainly kill their way of life. There will be no more ferry family. On top of that, he has enough headaches fighting with Beefy labor union.

Beefy Cow couldn't afford losing his job as ship builder for long either. Competing with the Regular Cow, the union worker has no chance, and at home, Milky Cow is mad at Beefy for not bringing home the bacon. Sacred Cow is all talk, eating from the sweat of Beefy.

Mad Cow didn't want to be a trouble maker. But when he saw so much corruption and government waste, he complained. Nobody listened. Getting mad seemed to be the only way to get Cowpalace's attention.

Of course, many Mad Cows are now changing party to the Holy Cow gang.

Holy Cow wonders what's wrong with Sacred Cow. Building a bridge is the only reliable way to make the connection with Everland. No more weather problems, ferry union worker strikes, or ramp break downs. Sure way to keep tourism alive.

He is trying to save Cowpalace from its dwindling population and shrinking businesses. Once a tourist's green haven, Cowpalace is now close to being a desert. What's wrong with building a bridge? Most people in Everland love it. Developers from other cities want it also.

Moo from KCOW 9 is struggling to report from inside the thicket of cheers and jeers.

The cork has been in the bottle so long that, once loosened, it pops. Unfortunately, their focus isn't on what they can do. Rather it is on what they want others to do. It will take a while before they begin to see themselves and others as one and the same cowmunity.

By this time, John, Buddy and Fluffy are all crowded in the front seat. Moo is giving them a very good description of the debate.

"Here is a true story," Billy Goat says. "A human friend of mine was looking for a RV. He saw an ad in the newspaper for a thirty-foot Sunseeker, four years old, with seven-thousand miles on it. The owner was selling it for $1,200. It sounded too good to be true, but he decided to follow up.

He made an appointment to see the RV, followed his GPS, and showed up at a beautiful home. A nice-looking lady in her fifties let him in.

She told him the RV was in excellent condition. Since the death of her husband, she didn't drive it at all. Curious, he asked "Is $1200 the price, not $12,000 or $ 24,000? She insisted that it would be sold at $1200.

"What's wrong with the RV?" He questioned. "Nothing" she replied.

He took the RV for a test drive. It ran perfectly. "Please tell me what's wrong with the RV." He asked.

"Nothing," she said. He bought the RV on the spot and paid her the $1200.

After she had filled out the pink slip and he had signed it, he pleaded with her again. "What wrong with the RV?" She replied, "My husband has written in his will that he wanted the money from this RV sale to go to his mistress."

You see, our position is not always the same as our true interest or concern. You and I know about Cowpalace's conflict and your position, but what is your common interest and concern? Let's talk about it."

And they talk. Hoofkerchief wiping, nose sniffing, and cows hugging.

John says, nodding and paws-holding Fluffy and Buddy, "Insight begins when you see your enemy is suffering. Love begins when you want their suffering to stop."

From Moo's comment, the assembly is a lot calmer. John also picks up some very good questions Billy is using:

"What happened to give you that impression?"

"What are the criteria for a good decision?"

"Can you tell me where you are coming from?"

He notices Billy tries to reframe blame into mutual contribution and restates intention into impact.

Moo reports that Billy acts like a traffic cop to direct the flow of communication, and stops those who violate the rules. When necessary, he lets people call for a time out to have a private coaching session. He calls a few sessions himself.

"Things seem to move along great." Moo says. It seems that everybody agrees job security is the main concern. If constant strikes, no resolution, and no new way of increasing tourism continue, Cowpalace will be dead in ten years. Everyone loses.

"Some worry too many tourists in town will threaten the way of life. How can we maintain the cow flavor–the slow pace of life in town and job security? Let's explore solutions that conclude with a better future."

Continuing his report, Moo says, "Many are tossing ideas into the discussion without any yelling as stated in the ground rules. Billy Goat is a good discussion traffic cop."

They are an hour into the forum.

"Let's make the ferry a floating museum and restaurant, and build the bridge. Everyone will have a job that way, in fact, more jobs than before. Ship builder, bridge builder, restaurant, gift shop owner—"

"What about the peaceful and quiet way of life that we enjoy?"

"There is no perfect answer, and something has to give. Maybe we can divide the town into residential and business areas to keep the best of the two worlds. A good business center around the bridge and a residential area around the west side of town."

Two hours pass. The future has just arrived.

"To celebrate this breakthrough from breakdown," the mayor says, "let's call off the strike and schedule a meeting to flesh out the details in this major project. Mr. Goat, will you do that?"

Act 5: Scene 3: Reconciliation

John is ready to see his dad. He is eager to tell him what he has wanted to say since long ago, when he became a Christian, and he wants to be reconciled with Uncle Robert and Aunt Suzie. In preparation, he adds these 3 EC ways to resolve conflict to his conflict tool-box, while waiting on Wise-owl:

Conflict is inevitable
Need determines fit
Triage conflict with Color ID
Manage conflict with 3 Rs
Resolve conflict in 3EC ways.

Then he goes through his notes and takes inventory of what he has just learned.

1. Conflict is inevitable; it is how we manage it that matters.

2. Your need and the others' need and the time frame will determine whether you choose *avoid*, *compel*, *negotiate*, *accommodate* or *collaborate*.

3. Triage the intensity of conflict by decoding the use of language and the intended goal.

4. CPR means *Conflict*, *Player* and *Roadmap*. The most critical issue is how well the players regulate anxiety. That will determine the nature of the fight.

5. To manage conflict you can use *Return*, (return monkey to their back) *Restrain* (first do no harm), and *Resolve* (turn conflict into dispute).

6. To resolve conflict you apply the 3EC ways: Explain *Conflict*, Extract *Concern* and Explore *Conclusion*.

Buddy and Fluffy seem to get along fine after some open and heartfelt dialogue. Wise-owl has given them good coaching on conflict management these two days.

Ultimately, it is the love and understanding they have found in each other that helps. Perhaps the sharing of pains and suffering instead of blame has cleared the path to healing.

You cannot legislate whipping. By force you can take the whip from their hands, but you cannot, by force, take the whip from their hearts.

Getting stuck together with minimal avoidance has enabled them to confront what needs confronting, to heal what needs healing, and to understand what needs understanding.

Fluffy says, "John, I've been a real jerk. Sorry I am always doing my own thing. I'm wired to be independent. Actually, ever since being abandoned in a cat alley, I dare not trust anyone anymore.

"Hearing 'the 101 ways to skin a cat' doesn't make me feel too safe, either. But I should be more considerate of your need without you having to worry about me and Buddy."

"Sorry too, John." Buddy says. "Guess I am so insecure because I think you don't like me anymore because you brought Fluffy home. I didn't realize you have an agonizing time running this new church. People have been very malicious. You have a handful."

Come to think about it. "*Abandon,*" "*cat alley,*" "*insecure,*" *—These are heavy loads to carry. Perhaps they are not roaring lions but wounded lambs.*

I should stand in awe at the load they carry, but instead I stand in judgment of how they carry them.

John gives the dog and cat a big bear hug.

Road Sign

"A problem adequately stated is a problem well on its way to being solved." R. Buckminster Fuller

Check Compass

How open have I been in listening to others' concerns?

What can I do to resolve our problem with the three EC ways?

Act 6:

Peace at Last—Transforming Conflict.

Act 6: Scene 1: A Look in the Mirror

"Fuffly and Buddy, can you wait here a minute? I need to run over to the terminal to check on the ferry schedule."

Roaring lions, wounded lambs. Is there something more than what we see in the faces of conflict?

Is growing up poor and despised and being nice to others just a way to avoid more problems, and to hide the lack of confidence? Is he, himself the newly discovered wounded lamb?

Can he make peace with his past, with himself?

Can he learn from Billy Goat to deal with conflict and with himself in an assertive, confident, respectful, and healthy manner?

Looking out at these gorgeous mountains and the blue river, aware that God has created them, John understands how He must have, in love, created him. So why the insecurity? He should know better.

He straightens up, looks towards heaven, and recites and affirms his beloved scriptures:

Psalm 139: 13-14 "For you created my inmost being, you knit me together in my mother's womb. I praise you because I am fearfully and wonderfully made; your works are wonderful, I know that full well."

And Jeremiah 29:11 says "For I know the plans I have for you,' declares the Lord, 'plans to prosper you and not to harm you, plans to give you hope and a future."

"I guess we all have problems. Me, Dad and Uncle Robert. Yes, even those people at church who want to hurt me. I imagine God loves them too. Please help me to forgive and forget."

"You are the potter. I'm the clay. Please do with me as you wish, Lord." Though the experiences are still painful, he takes comfort knowing all these will serve a bigger purpose as part of the whole.

He takes a panoramic view of his family from years past to the present turmoil with his church. He knows these problems are just groundwork for the eternal peace yet to come.

To forgive is not to forget the past, but to forge a better future.

Right out of the blue sky comes something flying toward him. Is it a plane, is it a bird, is it . . . Wise-owl! With a limp!

Act 6: Scene 2: Are We There Yet?

"Sorry John, your father has just passed away," Wise-owl says.

Time stands still. A whole life has just swept before his eyes. He missed the chance to say the final goodbye. *Can I find peace? Will dad find peace?*

Wise-owl flutters his wings to gain balance on John's shoulder while steadying the package around his neck.

"When I read him your letter, he pointed me to this book by his pillow. He wanted you to have it." With difficulty, Wise-owl unloads the package.

John opens the small, worn, leather-bound Bible. Right in the middle of the flyleaf, it reads:

> To Fred, a dear brother in the Lord. "If you hold to my teaching, you are really my disciples. Then you will know the truth, and the truth will set you free." John 8:31, 32.

We are glad to have you as our newest member at church. Happy birthday! Love in Christ.

Benny"

John heads back to his Sienna mini-van, hugging his father's *Bible* close to his heart.

He holds even more tightly the images of jumping, hitting, and catching bubbles his father blew for him on his fifth birthday. Though his dad couldn't afford to buy him a cake, playing with him was enough to make John remember forever the distant laughter.

"I love you Lord, and I lift my voice. To worship you…" John remembers this song of praise with a lump in his throat.

"Therefore we do not lose heart. Though outwardly we are wasting away, yet inwardly we are being renewed day by day. For our light and momentary troubles are achieving for us an eternal glory that far outweighs them all.

"So we fix our eyes not on what is seen, but on what is unseen. For what is seen is temporary, but what is unseen is eternal." (2 Corinthians 4:16-18.)

"Are we there yet?" Buddy and Fluffy ask together.

Slowly, word by word, with a solemn smile, John says, "Yes, and beyond."

John ends his mental notes on conflict with an addition:

Conflict is inevitable.

Combat is optional.

Collaboration is optimal.

Transformation is possible

Eternal peace is available.

"Thanks," He mutters. Wise-owl disappears into an old stack of conflict resolution notes and his beloved *Bible*.

"Goodbye, dad, see you in the morning." John says.

Road sign

The weak can never forgive. Forgiveness is the attribute of the strong. Mahatma Gandhi

Check Compass

Have I ever learned to forgive myself?

Who should I forgive?

Major's Log: To Pastors with Love.

Church fights: chances are you have one, are having one, or are heading toward one. Chances are our theology shames us, our peers avoid us, and our boss hassles us. But to those not reduced to ashes nor hardened beyond feeling, there is life, hope, and redemption, after a fight.

Right in the crossfire, it is easy to think you are the ignition switch and the center of every inferno. You smell the smoke oozing out from you. You sink into self-doubt and pity. The scorching heat is unbearable, the gossip is deafening, and your friends are awfully quiet. Hope is the last thing you see.

But most of the time, what I find at the core are people struggling to regulate their anxiety in response to a current event or a wounded past. Emotion overpowers logic. The wounded lamb becomes a well-intentioned dragon or a roaring lion.

Many times, you play only a very small part of the problem.

To gain some perspective, we need to draw a healthy boundary around us, between the war and the warriors. We also need to look past pain and anger, theirs and ours, past the now into ten years from now. The fact is, nothing, absolutely nothing on earth, is permanent. This too shall pass.

New growth can come out of the ashes. We can regain our footing and get steadier in our walk and clearer in our vision. Perhaps, we may even love people back to the Kingdom.

Sometimes we can't. Sometimes it is the situation and sometimes we are our own worst enemy, but in every conflict, we can learn something and do something about ourselves that we were previously unaware of. We can either change the conflict or be changed by it. Better or bitter, stumbling blocks or stepping stones—it is our choice.

Not long ago, a lady called me for a reference check on Melissa. A floodgate of hurtful memories of her betrayal, gossip, and slander opened up. Reading the anonymous letters from her to several persons demanding my head still gave me pain.

As her employer I have salvaged her job, and as her pastor I have cared for her and her family. Or so I thought.

Why would someone seemingly be so nice be so mean? I couldn't figure out where I went wrong.

She has settled down in another state and is applying for a job. "Would you recommend her for the position?" the caller asked. With that, I knew my time to get even had arrived.

I paused and I prayed. I believed she was qualified for this new job. That was only fair. But my pain resurged.

"Yes. She should do a good job."

God is a wonderful God.

The need for conflict resolution:

Politicians are satisfied with fifty-one percent of the vote, yet we feel awful if one out of a hundred people criticizes us and throws us into self-doubt and anguish.

Conflict disturbs our sleep, rattles our cage, and injures our image and ego. We worry more about putting out brush fires than igniting the church's flame. The dragons have won. The ministry has lost. No wonder we avoid, ignore, deny, or suppress conflict. But we cannot outlaw, exterminate, or exile it.

Direct conflict can easily burst into open flame and force us to bring on the hoses immediately, whether we like it or not. Latent conflict is unpleasant but bearable, risky and difficult to control but easy to let go.

So in the face of milder conflict, we see without seeing, hear without listening, touch without feeling. We look the other way.

As a popular song goes, "No one there, to disturb the sound of silence."©

Unfortunately, such conflict is infinitely patient and knows its time will come to the surface, possibly at the worst of times. At best, it creates a barrier to relationships and adds a burden to productivity. It can also simmer to a boil and even, sometimes, spill into catastrophe.

On May 2, 2003 the Associated Press stated of Sweden, Maine, "Residents of this potato farming community pride themselves on the safety of their close-knit town, now are scared and shocked after fatal arsenic poisoning at a church luncheon. ...The case was declared a homicide Thursday . . ." ©

Why didn't people see the smoke before the explosion?

Seldom does conflict cause body counts, but often it causes a loss of vision, enthusiasm, perspective, and outreach. Church growth is only as good as church health, and, in part, church health is only as good as managing conflict.

On 9/11, humanity received a wakeup call. Blood flowed and our nation mourned. The terrorists marched on and still march on.

We can no longer afford to leave conflict resolution to the Pentagon, the police department, or the courthouse. The fact is, we all are capable of committing violent acts ourselves.

We must understand the nature of conflict, and put in place management before another church growth conference, another pastor resignation, another lawsuit, or another mass exit of members. Building a fifty-dollar fence in front of a cliff is much easier and less costly than building a fifty-million-dollar hospital below it.

Managing church or personal conflict needs guts, not blood. It is not for the faint at heart. No Geneva Convention has established rules for how much firepower is appropriate in a church fight, nor is there any over-the-counter drug to create forgiveness. The crossfire will burn scars in our heart, and wrestling with it will put a limp in our walk, but we must try.

We must remind ourselves that "success is not final and failure is not fatal. It is the courage to continue that counts." (Winston Churchill) and "I will repay you for the years the locusts have eaten" (Joel 2:25). Joseph affirmed the outcome

"You intended to harm me, but God intended it for good." (Gen 50:20). God is a gracious God.

Before you can wipe the tears of others, you need to weep first. When the battle cry nags me through many sleepless nights, I know there will be the sound of redemption across the valley of death. When I gaze into the dark lifeless sky and listen to the songs of the night, I know dawn is just on the horizon.

When my eyes go blurry, and I think, *God, I don't want to be a pastor any more*, I know someday, somehow, somewhere, those difficult times will become the most precious of all.

God makes everything new and beautiful in His time.

The greater the conflict, the greater the pain, the greater the transformation. Jesus displayed boundless love, mercy, and grace on the cross at Calvary. He transformed law into grace, the temporal into eternal, and tragedy into triumph. God's agenda is not only to sustain us when we are in pain, but also to redeem and transform us through it.

"And we know that in all things God works for the good of those who love him, who have been called according to His purpose." Roman 8:28

Ralph Waldo Emerson once said, "When it is dark enough, men see the stars."

Part of the miracle of grace is that broken vessels can be made whole, with ever greater capacity than before. So be not anxious for anything, but in all things give thanks. God is in control.

Ultimately in the long and broad scheme of things, being a pastor is the highest calling from God Almighty, the compassionate One we can call "Abba". He loves us, and will equip, sustain, and transform those He calls.

Take courage. This too shall pass, and victory is on the horizon.

Road Sign

We find comfort among those who we agree with us – growth among those who don't. Frank A. Clark

Epilogue: Are We There Yet— Fuel for Your Journey

Life is tough, and sometimes it seems hopeless. After fights you wonder; can Johnny ever change? Can *I* change? Is there any hope for us?

Saul was furious on the way to Damascus, clinching his fist, grabbing the arrest warrant, spewing curses, and ready to stone to death those who had conflicts with his belief.

For him, combat was the only option, but God pulled him to the other extreme—transformation.

In Damascus, after that blazing light from heaven that blinded him for three days and knocked him off the donkey, God transformed him from a sinner to a saint, a hater to a lover, from forming conflict to being transformed by it. Finally he was martyred for the thing he had spent his whole life fighting, until then.

"But the Lord stood at my side and gave me strength, so that through me the message might be fully proclaimed, and all the Gentiles (those he used to despise and wanted to kill) might hear it." 2 Timothy 4:17

Wow!! There is hope for me. These are the words of a changed man, at peace with God, with his enemies and with himself.

We were thirty-five thousand feet over Greece, Turkey, and the Mediterranean Sea, agonizing over the possibility of seeing any changes in those we loved, carrying the pain of a parent, a grandparent, a pastor, and a friend, searching for hope in the ruins my wife and I were about to see.

For fourteen days we traced the footsteps of Paul among cities and city ruins, shorelines and ocean, mountains and valleys. Paul travelled on foot, on a donkey treading through the unforgiving terrains, and in a boat buffeted by wind and wave, carrying basic necessities. We were cocooned in an air-conditioned bus, sitting on soft cushions, carrying a camera.

I tried to connect the past with the present, the temporal with the eternal, and the conflict with its transformation.

I've concluded that the greatest culprit and source of all conflict transcend time, space, culture, and circumstances. They come from the tug of war between good and evil, my way and His way, who I want to be and who God intends me to be. This DNA of ours that causes us to break loose from God we call self-centeredness, sin, and pride.

From the moment we first cry, squeeze our tiny fists, and stomp our pinkish feet, right out of our mother's womb, we struggle in this land of *between*, we try to prove our self-worth by increasing our net-worth— what we have and do, instead of who we are in His sight.

To bridge the gap between God and us, we try possession, power, position, and philosophy. But these are just symptoms of our wish to be at home with the Creator. It is a vacuum that needs no fixing, but needs filling by the Holy Spirit. *Salvation*. Something only God can give and by choice, we can receive.

"For it is by grace you have been saved, through faith- and this is not from yourselves, it is the gift of God- not by works, so that no one can boast." Ephesians 2:8, 9

Once Paul accepted that gift of salvation, he bridged that gap. He crossed the chasm. He filled a gaping hole somewhere deep in his life, an itch he could not scratch. A whole new world opened up to him. It was like the astronaut who looked at the planet earth the first time. His perspective changed. Life had meaning and dignity, plan and purpose, origin and destiny.

Out of this change comes the ability to forgive others and ourselves. It opens the door for the ultimate transformation. The real conflict resolution. Oh, how we need to change and overcome our internal conflict. God is in the business of doing that, if we let him.

Over thirty-five years as pastor, I have seen and befriended many changed people whose stories breathe life into my own circumstances, and give me hope.

Let's turn angry fists into compassionate hands. Let's stand in awe at the burden what others carry, and not in judgment how they carry it.

Keep on praying. People can change. The person you have in mind may surprise you someday.

Prayer for Peace

LORD, make me an instrument of Your peace.

Where there is hatred, let me sow love;

where there is injury, pardon;

where there is doubt, faith;

where there is despair, hope;

where there is darkness, light;

and where there is sadness, joy.

O Divine Master,

Grant that I may not so much seek

to be consoled as to console;

to be understood as to understand;

to be loved, as to love;

for it is in giving that we receive,

it is in pardoning that we are pardoned,

and it is in dying that we are born to eternal life.

The Franciscans

Road Sign

"To forgive is to set a prisoner free and discover that the prisoner was you." Lewis B. Smades

Thank You

Time is your most precious asset; far more valuable than the money you have spent buying this book. I thank you for sharing such precious time with me.

For those wanting to explore and expand the experience of slaying conflict and healing souls, go to "Let's Huddle" as a group or individual. You will open greater windows of wonder, mercy and grace.

Peacemaking is my passion. Over thirty years I have seen many lives changed. If I can be of help, please write me with comments or questions.

I'd be glad to hear from you. Would you also share your success stories with me?

Agapeace4u@gmail.com

In the age of 9/11,

Class Warfare and Occupy Movement,

The new frontier of conflict is none of these

But the battle of the soul.

"Behold, I stand at the door and knock; if anyone hears My voice and opens the door, I will come in to him and will dine with him, and he with Me." Rev 3:20

Let's Huddle

Act 1: The Journey Begins — Defining Conflict.

What stands out in this scene?

Explain what "silence is not golden when you are in pain" means.

What does "more people are hurting than you know" say to us?

What are some of the trivial things people are fighting for in churches?

Do you agree with the definition of *conflict* given? What kind of examples of conflict can you give?

What is a *mental container*? Any examples?

What kind of internal conflict have you experienced?

Give an example of "leveling the playing field"

What is the difference between appeasement and peacemaking?

What is the difference between forgiving and denying?

Explain and give examples of the statement "in conflict you confront who you are, who you are not, and who you want to be?"

Act 2: Dogsville — Responding to Conflict.

What's wrong with Buddy hanging around John like a leash?

What's your take on "needs determine fit"? Any examples?

Have you ever chosen avoidance? If so, why?

John says 'Maybe the dogs hate the cats because they see something they don't like about themselves in the cats." Any comment? Any example?

Can you give some examples of negotiating, collaborating, and accommodating?

What is your response to the "needs determine fit" model?

What current church situation can you apply the "needs determine fit principle" to?

What do you think about the "Road Sign" quote from Edwards Noyes Wescott?

Act 3: Cat fight — Triaging Conflict.

What is the difference between directly involving yourself with a *conflict* and managing a *conflict*?

Any comment on "conflict is not a single event but an emotional process"?

What are some of the ways to escalate or de-escalate conflict?

What are some of the ways to decode meaning?

What have you learned from this scene?

Why are snipers so deadly? How do you handle them?

Can you give some examples of *containment*?

Are there times when *containment* or *restrain* is wrong?

What other words beside "calm down" that can produce an opposite result in de-escalating conflict?

What is the difference between active and passive containment?

Please give examples of how to "level the playing field."

Why is the legal process unable to deal with hatred, intolerance, and other moral issues?

What is the difference between *position* and *interest*?

What is the most important tool you can use to deal with conflict?

Act 4: Motel CPR — Decoding the DNA of Conflict.

Give some examples of church conflicts that are not about right and wrong, but about lack of appreciation and respect, or lack of acknowledgement of differences?

Give some examples of *value conflicts* at church, at home, and at the national and international level?

Can you give examples of *polarity conflict*?

What is the first thought that comes to your mind when you see the word *conflict*?

Can you share some thoughts on *self-differentiation*?

Please name some bad roadmaps.

What would you do to uncover those bad roadmaps?

Act 5: Cowpalace—Managing Conflict.

What are some of the sources of generational conflict?

What are the alternatives to conflict resolution?

Can you give examples of how *position* is not the same as *interest*?

Please tell us why, "insight begins when you see your enemy is suffering, and love begins when you want it stop"?

What insight have you gained from this act?

Act 6: Peace at Last—Transforming Conflict

Why did John say in respond to the question "are we there yet?" with "Yes, and beyond."?

What is a good way to disturb the sound of silence?

What is the difference between our self-worth and net-worth?

What is the greatest conflict resolution?

Who is a peacemaker?

What three practical tools or insights have you gained from this book?

A call to action

Conflict affects individuals but often involves groups as well. Let me quote a song written by Commissioner Dick Krommenhoek as a corporate call to action for peace.

Use me, Jesus, as you need

Here immersed in holy splendor, I am kneeling at
your feet, offering you a full surrender; use me, Jesus,
as you need.

Young girls forced to sell their bodies, trafficked from across the globe. Through their suffering Jesus calls me to bring justice, love and hope.

There's a teen who's filled with anger, lacking love that comprehends. Though on Face-book and on Twitter, Christ needs me to be his friend.

When I see a desperate mother with a child who's high on speed, can I say 'Why should I bother?' what more calling do I need?

So much loneliness around us, people dying, no-one knows. I must live the love of Jesus, caring, bearing, being close.

All those millions who are not yet saved by God's amazing grace, need to hear the Saviour's message, so I'll give him all my days.

Commissioner Dick Krommenhoek Territorial Commander Finland and Estonia Territory

Stories of Hope

Rick and I began our marriage by building what many call the American Dream, house, cars, vacations, and stuff. *Lots of stuff.* But, we built that life on good times, fast fun, and lifestyle full of substance abuse. By 1994 it was apparent, living life our way was not working and, pregnant with our second child, we separated. I struggled to stay clean, feeling empty and very alone.

What I knew about God was very basic. My mother encouraged me to go to church with friends and I would come home and tell her all about what the services were like. Mom had cancer and life had alterations, but Mom did pray and I knew about prayer. So, when I found myself alone, I thought about God and asked, "Where are you God and why aren't you helping me?" In my heart I heard a small still voice, "Because you haven't asked."

So I prayed the only words I could muster, "Lord, please help me." Four small words led to a flood of tears and a river of confessions. On my knees, I spoke of pain, anger, sorrow, and regrets, I cried out to the Father I never really sought to know, the One who I had shut out long ago and in His grace, He met me where I was. I surrendered my heart to the One who knew every sin and loved me anyway.

I began attending church and I remember beginning my Bible reading at John. Life was not easy, but God is trustworthy. In John 16:33 Jesus says, "I have told you these things, so that in me you may have peace. In this world you will have trouble. But take heart! I have overcome the world." I took Him at His word.

After three years of separation, Rick contacted me wanting to see his children. God had been at work in his life as well. Rick had entered The Salvation Army Adult Rehabilitation Center in Riverside County. The man came back walking in Christ! It wasn't long before our family was re-united and we were blessed with our third daughter, Samantha.

Life is so unpredictable. In March of 2010, I was diagnosed with colon cancer. Remembering John 16:33 "In me you may have peace" I would go through surgery and chemotherapy in His strength. He carried me into every surgery, every test, and each treatment. Today I celebrate 3 years and

7 months cancer-free to the glory of God. His peace has continued to be my comfort. God Is faithful!

Today Rick and I are enjoying lives of restoration with 35 years of marriage, 16 years of sobriety; with three beautiful daughters and granddaughters ALL to the glory and honor of God. As Cadets of The Salvation Army College, we are praying and training to be a vehicle for His Word and a tool in His hand.

Cadet Edith Dye-Mabie The Salvation Army College for Officer Training Western Territory USA

My Mom and Dad were married and divorced to each other five times and are divorced now. Before I was eighteen we had moved thirteen times. By the time I turned eighteen it only took me two weeks to move out even though I was still in my senior year in High School. I was going to do things different and no one could stand in my way.

With the good work ethic my Dad and Mom had taught me it wasn't long before I had the best job our little town could offer someone my age. I finished high school, with honors, and decided to head back to California. The place we had left against my will four years earlier.

Once back in California I quickly landed a union job and made enough start up cash and connections to start my own landscaping business with a friend. We did great and grew to sixty accounts in less than a year! All this while holding down a forty hour a week warehouse job! It was also during this time I was introduced to some habits that would later prove uncontrollable.

After some shared owner/operator struggles sending me and a friend our separate ways I decided to move into the Locksmith trade. In about seven years I was able to go on my own, and before I knew it I was making more money than I knew was possible. From that point forward I was able to live in houses with ocean views, own more cars than I had licensed drivers, and as far as I was concerned I had everything my heart wanted or needed.

Then life hit, the good and the bad of it. Life hurled me some rough patches and I returned to some addictions and habits that I had, until now, been able to reserve to the weekends and only in moderation. After all they had always given me the confidence and energy needed to press on during rough times in the past. My Mom had, with the help of the good Lord, turned her life around during my childhood. From that she had taught me some good ways to cope. I tried to turn to the Good Book and find Jesus, but found the alcohol and drug a quicker and cleaner cure to what ailed me.

The self-mediated approach did work well at first, but not for long. In the matter of about three years I had lost it all. For the next four years I would find myself wondering homeless, on the streets.

I did things I said I'd never do. Sometimes going up to three days without food I would resort to whatever I could find, even if that meant the last few fries or bite of someone's hamburger in my neighborhood restaurant trash can.

I was hopeless. Holding on to the street life and all its poisons numbed the feelings. The more comfortable I got in that life the more I was diminishing as a person. I had become a shell of a man. I had nowhere to go. Not even my family would take my calls and rightly so. I was a mess.

The good news is The Salvation Army took a chance on me when no one else would. I received not only help for my medical and physical sickness, love when I was unlovable, but salve for my soul.

What I freely received I now am motivated by the love of God to freely give away! My wife and I have the privilege of serving alongside an amazing team here at the local Salvation Army, helping over 1,400 people each week.

Even more during the holidays! I could work the rest of my days giving back and still owe The Salvation Army for saving my life.

Lt. Paul Swain Salvation Army

Monterey Peninsula, CA

About The Author

Major Eric Kam Wah Lo has worked as a growing expert on Conflict Resolution for over thirty years. He graduated from California State University as a Civil Engineer, and earned a teaching degree from Sir Robert Black College of Education in Hong Kong. He was a pastor and administrator in The Salvation Army. He is a certified mediator.

He has made peace between two feuding Native American tribal leaders, merged an American National Organization local chapter with The Salvation Army local chapter, resurrected a church destroyed by legal problems, mediated disputes through his Agapeace ministry, and written articles on church conflict and cross cultural issues for *The Officer* magazine, circulated in 125 countries.

He retired in 2013, and he and his wife Cheryl tour the United States in their RV full time. They have two children, Ethan and Bethany, and granddaughter, Kalia.

Slaying Conflict, Healing Souls

Are We There Yet?

Five Steps to Real Peace Now

Book Order Form

To order a copy of this book, please call 805-827-5198 or email Eric at <u>Agapeace4u@gmail.com</u> and provide the following information:

Your name: _____

Address: _____

City: _____ State: ___ Zip Code: _____

Telephone: _____ Date of Order _____

Signature: _____

\# of Books _____ x $18.99 per book plus shipping and handling

Total of check or money order: _____

This book is available at special quantity discounts for bulk purchases for promotions, premiums, fund-raising, or education use.

CPSIA information can be obtained at www.ICGtesting.com
Printed in the USA
BVOW10s1623081214

378223BV00004B/16/P